ALTERED GRACE

A. TACKED

authorHOUSE®

AuthorHouse™
1663 Liberty Drive
Bloomington, IN 47403
www.authorhouse.com
Phone: 1 (800) 839-8640

Published by AuthorHouse   01/13/2017

ISBN: 978-1-5246-5910-3 (sc)
ISBN: 9781-5246-5908-0 (hc)
ISBN: 978-1-5246-5909-7 (e)

Library of Congress Control Number: 2017900415

Print information available on the last page.

Any people depicted in stock imagery provided by Thinkstock are models,
and such images are being used for illustrative purposes only.
Certain stock imagery © Thinkstock.

This book is printed on acid-free paper.

Contents

Acknowledgments

In memory of all those unfortunate souls who crossed paths with Clayton and Beatrice. I pray you find peace and forgiveness. May your tortured souls be set free now and for eternity.

Clayton and Beatrice, I forgive you both. In order to live the life I prayed for, in letting you both go, I also must forgive you. May your tortured souls be set free as well.

To my siblings, both living and in spirit, please know you were never alone through it all. I pray your lives will be rich and full, and may your childhood demons be cast away forever. In your journeys, may love always find your doorsteps, and may hope be a staple in your homes.

Last but not least, for those of you unsure of the value of prayer, let me help set the record straight. I am a product of prayer. Through a child's eyes and understanding, praying to be "normal" was a simple request, a show of faith in a world I couldn't understand. I had a deep desire to remain whole, to remain with purpose. All the while, the world I lived in harbored nothing but pain and fear.

Regardless of what your higher self means to you, it is your fortress. Always believe in something bigger than yourself to see you through, and, my friends, your rainbows will always shine in the most brilliant colors.

After all, it is your birthright.

Always in memory, you will never be forgotten!

Love for eternity,
A. Tacked

Prologue

"Now I lay me down to sleep. I pray the Lord my soul to keep. If I should die before I wake, I pray the Lord my soul to take. Dear Father in heaven, do not let me die tonight. Most importantly, if I am to live, please, dear Father, keep me normal. Amen."

Night fell and grew silent. Just beyond where the mind disconnects, drifting apart from its awakened world into slumber, I sat and watched.

Restful sleep had never been a sure thing. Dreamless nights were rare gifts, far and few between. Here again, mixed with the sound of my shallow breaths resonating in the darkness, the footsteps of the powerful wolves could be heard making their way through the tall grass.

Tonight's procession had already begun.

The size of the wolf pack had increased over the years. Close to twenty majestic creatures traveled on any given night. Many of the wolves had thick, coarse coats of smoky-gray fur, while the remainder had fur as black as the night in which they traveled. Had it not been for their emerald-colored eyes illuminated like fireflies in the near moonless night, their shadows would have gone unnoticed, completely lost in the darkness.

Driving the evil away from the house, away from the innocent lambs inside, they fulfilled the pact delivered ages ago, when the lines between good and evil had been drawn. Honor was not something to be taken lightly.

It was not only the wolves' duty; it was their covenant, their burden to serve humankind. Like storm clouds forming, evil had become stronger; too many good people had sat idle. Those capable of making a difference had turned away; those of good intentions had been swallowed up, caught between the two worlds. The wolves had been brought in by a pure and higher power to balance the scales—to restore order in a disorderly world.

With barely a breath apart, the wolves followed tightly behind the lost souls as the lineup began to move forward across the field.

In stark contrast, the forms of the lost souls were hideous and vile.

Tragically lost, these creatures had once been human, perhaps even people of faith and reason. Greed and lust had made them easy targets, ready and willing to give it all for the sake of a good time. Making deals with the darkness, they had turned their backs on humankind, trading their hearts for lies and false promises. Now among the wolves, the lost souls stood, notably emaciated. Tall and gaunt, their spines curved severely outward.

Restricted movement over the centuries had caused deformation from lack of a consistent upright position. Hipbones jutted out, large and disproportionate, void of any cushiony muscular tissue. The noise made from the friction of a ball and socket gave off a disturbing clacking, rhythmic sound as their bodies in motion continued forward. With eyes protruding out of their sockets, the fixed, unmovable stare could not deny the shameful truth—they could no longer see.

It had been ingenious enlisting help from the wolves. God knew that wolves could endure long travels with few provisions. Knowing that some of the lost souls would regrettably return by morning to huddle alone beneath the cellar stairs or in the attic's corners, God, in his mercy, ensured the wolves would never give up. Night after night, they would make the sacrificial trek in hopes that even one soul might be saved by morning. Night after night in slumber, I too became part of their plan.

My name is Helen, and I am a lamb terrified by the shameful world around me. The wolves do not scare me nearly as much as the lost souls do. I find comfort and protection in the very same animals that scare other children with their inaccurate fairy tales of a red-caped girl visiting an unsuspecting grandmother—the better to eat you with, ha!

Beyond their myths, where truth becomes timeless, I am also the wolf.

Part 1

THE IMPENDING STORM

The saddest thing about betrayal is that it never
comes from your enemies. -Anonymous

Chapter 1

IN THE BEGINNING

The tiny house sat vacant, hidden from sight by cattails, tall weeds, and overgrown nettle—nature's barbed wire. Years had passed since the house had actually been lived in. Even then, it had only seen short-term tenants throughout the years, none staying long enough to warm the place with human touch. Looking more like a large shed than a house, it bore two rooms and a small porch, which had been added in hopes of giving it a homey look. The porch, really no more than a slab of cement, had cracked from harsh winters, causing it to lean to one side. This was nobody's home sweet home.

Standing outside after dusk, if you listened carefully, you could hear voices murmuring in the wind. An unsettling eeriness had long ago set up residence on the property. Lonely and abandoned, it would be a long while before it would see inhabitants other than the ones that had been living there in the shadows all along. As time marched on, years later, my family would inhabit the simple house tucked away in the cattails. Evil would be getting long-term houseguests, some it could relate to. Mama and Papa would be coming home.

I have waited more than thirty years to tell my story. Since the day I walked out of the front door and into the afternoon sunshine, free for the first time in my life, I knew this day would come. As I said good-bye to the innocent spirits still trapped, the ones that had comforted me for all those years, I knew this day would come. Time has a way of healing hearts that one would never believe could mend. I once lived under a paralyzing fear so powerful that even the deaths of those responsible couldn't give me true comfort. In their deaths, the path remains obscure at times.

Although the physical body dies when the heart beats no more, the demons can grow stronger.

Days, like the repetitive motion of a swinging pendulum, came and went. Remaining normal through it all became the only true goal, the precious pot of gold at the end of a blackened rainbow. Despair wrestled with hope. Sometimes the sinking feelings felt much like deep holes dug into the ground. I never knew when I might topple over or be pushed into the hole for all of eternity. I was forgotten and erased; survival can be a daunting task.

To understand my journey, I must now share with you theirs. Hurry, for the first collaborator is soon to be born.

Chapter 2

THE MAKINGS OF CLAYTON

The clock above the massive but lifeless four-burner cookstove sounded loudly. One, two, three identical piercing chimes all announced that three o'clock had arrived. Had it been like any other Sunday, three o'clock would have just come and gone, finding the relatives pleasantly dozing off in their chairs, digesting their full bellies of baked chicken and boiled potatoes.

Church by then would be neatly tucked away for yet another week, with each of the faithful feeling confident that the message from the priest was meant for him or her alone, a special one-on-one connection with the above. On this particular holy day, religion and hearty meals would have to be set aside. Three o'clock had come to announce a different reality, one tone each for humiliation, embarrassment, and contempt.

Although the curtains had been drawn not so much for privacy but as a sign of mourning, a life was taking shape in the dimly lit back bedroom. On a twin-size bed draped with a sheet of clear plastic, Linda lay screaming and perspiring. Each hard contraction made her body ripple in pain; it wouldn't be long now. Linda's mother stood across the room, glaring at her, arms held tightly to her own bulging belly, her fists clenched. It wasn't difficult to see that there would be no mother-daughter bonding here.

The air in the room was thick, a mixture of tension and raw adrenaline.

Would God show any mercy? How could he not turn away after witnessing such blasphemy? Had the devil already moved in to gloat over his latest conquest? Linda's provocative ways had caused all of this. A girl in full bloom had no business teasing men the way she had. She had silly notions of running away to a happily ever after with some man named Charlie. Where was Charlie now? Was he just another suitor who had easily managed to unbutton the front of Linda's dress? A man had a right to take whatever he felt was offered up to him, both at home and otherwise; women were supposed to know that. Linda was never short on invitations. Somebody had to teach her, and indeed he had.

As the final wave of labor pains bore down on Linda, one determined and exhaustive push expelled the seven-pound baby boy from Linda's previously swollen belly. She was finally free once again.

Clayton made his entry into the world as normal as any child could—born to a family who already hated him. Clayton's blue eyes and chestnut-colored hair were no match for the freedom that called to his mother. On that hot summer day in August, Clayton became the property of his grandparents.

Already ripe with child, Clayton's grandmother had been reeling from the morning sickness that had come on with a vengeance, leaving her tired and irritable. The news of her own pregnancy had come as a surprise at first.

It had been a long time since her children were in diapers. Now here she was with not only her own baby on the way at her age but saddled with her daughter's bastard child as well.

As if sensing he didn't belong, Clayton began his turbulent life with fitful bouts of colic. Day in and day out, his screams could be heard even through the heavy wooden door he stayed behind, alone, for most of his first several months. Those brilliant sky-blue eyes should have been able to look up and see loving eyes in return. Unfortunately, few knew of him, knew of the little boy left to himself to simply stare up into the ceiling.

On a frigid night in February, the baby who had been protected in the womb of Clayton's grandmother was born. Little Rosie came into the world, frail and listless. Her cry was weak and seemed buried within her chest. In reality, it was underdeveloped lungs that had sealed this child's fate even before her entry into the world. The 1930s hadn't heard of fancy equipment, the kind that could breathe life into a fragile newborn.

In the next few months, as the cold winter chill raged on and Clayton's colic became even more unbearable, poor little Rosie developed pneumonia.

With Rosie barely clinging to life, the spring weather came and brought with it winter's and her finality. Poor Rosie was dead before the spring thaw had made its way into the ground.

Hatred has a way of turning the heart to stone and further loss keeps that stone well-polished. Clayton, now a budding toddler, had become even more of a major inconvenience in his home of last resort.

With a loss too large to overcome, his grandparents set out to punish Clayton for Rosie's death, blaming Clayton for taking too much of their time away from the child they loved. It was time to make Clayton pay for being alive. First they would start with his name. They would never tell him his real name, the name they put on the birth certificate. It would be their little secret. Clayton hadn't earned an identity, and to them, he had stolen their little Rosie's identity anyway. Clayton had their last name because the law required it, but the first name, well, that was their choice. A fun little surprise when little Clayton became a man and didn't know who he really was.

LIVESTOCK

Seasons passed on the farm, and Clayton, in spite of it all, began to grow into his slender legs. A boy should think about baseball on lazy summer days, but Clayton's existence never lent itself to lazy days without chores.

Clayton milked the cows and tilled the farmland with both ox and plow.

Whenever the farm required it, Clayton mended the fences and performed any other maintenance that came along. His hands developed in spite of the raised calluses that blanketed them from the tips of his fingers to the center of his palms.

From sunup to sundown, it was an unspoken rule that he was to remain out of sight and hard at work. Forgiveness for being a burden to his grandparents was never forthcoming. Each day helped to fuel their deep regret for taking in such a waste of life. They never looked directly at Clayton because it only caused the memory of their dead daughter to come rushing in all over again. Clayton never knew the warmth of a hug or felt the pride of a well-deserved pat on the back. Even landing on the honor roll at the elementary school he attended in town didn't earn him a simple "Atta boy!" or an extra serving at the supper table. Clayton continued to grow physically, but his compassion for living things began to diminish and shrink with each insult and each welt from his grandfather's belt.

As the seasons passed, Clayton spent more time out in the barn, tending to the livestock. He began to sleep in the barn, as it always felt safer away from the house, away from people. He learned not to feel any attachment to the cows he shared a stall with. Given his situation, attachment was not an easy or natural task anyway. After all, like everything else in his world, cows had a practical purpose, and once they felt the hammer on their skull, then their purpose had come full circle. Nothing more, nothing less.

One summer, Clayton broke his "no attachments" rule. A stray dog wandered onto the farm, and Clayton decided to keep him and name him Pal.

Pal was skin and bones and looked about as broken as Clayton felt. He made the mistake of getting too close to that scrawny mutt. A feeling came over him that made him uncomfortable. He liked to be in Pal's company.

Somehow that dumb dog didn't care if he treated him well or not. Even after a kick or two, Pal would call it a truce and come love on him. Granddad shot the dog later that summer when he suspected that it was killing the chickens.

The sound of the gun that ended poor Pal's world made Clayton dig his fingers into his own skin. He wouldn't feel that way about anything or anyone ever again. It was clear to him now that he was just biding time until he could get to hell out of there.

Clayton, like any kid being raised in the North Country in the 1930s, packed a shotgun like today's teens tote cell phones. He learned to shoot before he was actually physically strong enough to lift the gun to his shoulder. Clayton self-taught himself to shoot from the hip, as it was the most comfortable for him. His eerie accuracy was the only encouragement he needed, and soon he was practicing his aim whenever he had time away from chores. As he practiced, first with tin cans, old glass bottles, and cardboard, he became increasingly confident in his ability to hit whatever was put in front of him. It wasn't long before targets that moved were his favorite. Once the squirrels and rabbits became boring, Clayton started to take a liking to the stray cats that he would find out behind the barn.

He knew that they would make a fierce screeching sound if he just nicked them enough to get their attention. Watching them howl and carry on was more fun than when the game was done and he put a bullet between their eyes.

It wasn't long before his grandfather assigned Clayton a nickname, his new calling card. "You long-legged, peak'ed-nose son of a bitch." This insult seemed to make the old man happy, and he used it every chance he got.

One more reminder of how much Clayton was hated cut through him like a knife cuts through butter. In time, however, the pain of abuse stung less and a newfound feeling of adrenaline and pure hatred replaced the fear that drove him.

From time to time, his real mother would come pay a visit to her parents.

It was at those times that she would look through Clayton as if he weren't actually even there. Only when she threatened him with a horrible punishment if he didn't stop being such a tremendous burden to her parents did she even regard him as being there, worthy of her voice at all.

As Clayton became a teenager, he suspected that Granddad was urinating in his milk. The only time a smile would come over the old man's face was when he watched to make certain that all of the milk was drained from Clayton's glass—a new house rule. The color and the rancid taste became clues of the wickedness that caused the old man so much pleasure.

The belt had become less intimidating as Clayton, being a boy of almost sixteen, had outgrown the fear of a good lashing. The fist became the punishment of choice, and Clayton felt the brunt of being clocked on many occasions. Sometimes, he would actually laugh after another split lip. It seemed old Granddad was losing what it took to really administer a solid punch.

On one particularly bad night, caught between the growing pains of becoming a man and another beating in the barn, Clayton was hit for the final time. As the old man's fist landed on his bottom lip, barely healed from the last beating, Clayton spit out a mouthful of blood. He then rolled his tongue across the split to taste the hot, sweet blood that oozed its way down the front of his flannels. Somehow, the taste had sexually aroused him.

The adrenaline rush made his heart race. He had really tasted blood, and now, as he licked its stickiness away from his teeth, he yelled with an intoxicating vengeance inside of him, "You're the long-legged, peak'ed-nose son of a bitch, and next time, the blood won't be my own!"

Chapter 4

BERRIES BY THE TRACKS

Clayton's story started with him as an infant and progressed. Seems like Beatrice's should also. Unfortunately, Beatrice began as the property of her older sisters with little mention of her biological parents during the early, formidable years. She was just another mouth to feed in an oversized family short on love and long on neglect, lost in the shuffle of chores and busy days.

Beatrice reached for another of the succulent berries that temporarily lay hidden beneath the leaves of the bushes. Oh, how she loved blackberries. It was excruciating not to ram all of the tender morsels into her mouth as her belly rumbled its confession of a skimpy breakfast. *Ma needs the money*, she thought as she dutifully placed each berry carefully in the wicker basket that was probably as old as she was. It was a good season for picking, and she relished the fact that no other competition knew about the berry bushes that grew just shy of the railroad tracks into town. It was her perfect heaven. It didn't bother her much that she was actually about a mile into the wooded land that weaved itself around the plot of ground she called home. A few times, she had stumbled onto a bear and had to leave her baskets behind only to have to go back minutes later to retrieve the lost baskets, emptied of berries, before she sulked home.

One particular afternoon, as she was heading home just before suppertime, she witnessed something that she would never forget, nor could she tell anyone at home. An enormous black, V-shaped shadow came up from behind her, so close that she could feel its breath on the back of her neck.

The scent was a mixture of hot urine and sulfur, much like the smell that a strike from a match on sandpaper makes. In the limited glimpse that Beatrice allowed herself, the oversized flying creature almost looked like an incredibly large flying monkey, not that she had ever seen one before to compare it to. With her hands up to cover her nose and then to cover the scream that was begging to come out from her throat, Beatrice shut her eyes tightly and hoped that she could disappear from sight. Feeling a sudden whooshing gust, she cautiously peeked through the slits of her closed eyes just in time to see the back end of this strange intruder take flight over her head, disappearing into the sky. She had never been so scared, nor had she ever seen such a frightening sight. No one would believe her story, and they would likely punish her for making up tales, so she decided that she would keep it to herself and be very careful from that afternoon forward.

Beatrice didn't have time for playing with dolls and such. As decided by her mother, a formidable and strictly practical woman with little use for love and compassion, Beatrice was responsible for picking, cleaning, and selling berries, whatever the season and whatever berry was ripe at the time.

There would be no discussion about it that a girl of her age, nearly eight, shouldn't be able to contribute and help pay for her way in the family.

Beatrice never questioned why a family of twelve, who barely had enough food on the supper table, would be so willing to sell these delicious treats for a dime a quart or a quarter a bucket. She, her five sisters, and her four brothers each had a specific role in the family, whether it be tending to the younger children, doing wash for the neighbors for a quarter a basket load, cooking meals, cleaning laundry on the old wringer washer, or cleaning the house. Each of them knew his or her place and didn't dare question the inevitable.

It went without saying that during Lent, Pa would spare the bottle. It was never clear as to whether or not he thought this act of piety would ensure him a place in heaven or if this vacation from evil would outsmart the demons that plagued his dreams. Nevertheless, like good, strong Catholics, Pa and the family said the rosary together as one big, faithful family each night through Lent.

Beatrice thought back to a time when she and her siblings had split the duty tending the fields and gardens. The last two years, Beatrice's pa had drunk up the seed money and the gardens became overgrown with weeds and brush. Beatrice's ma never obligated herself to any explanation of why she hadn't taken on any of the chores. Perhaps she felt entitled to a break while her husband worked as a letter carrier, ironically a letter carrier who never learned to read. Maybe she needed to save up her energy for the almost nightly beatings that she received from him. Pa liked the bottle, and it seemed that for every swig he took, it was another backhander for Ma. Many nights, Pa would grab Beatrice's mother by the back of the head and drag her across the old wooden floors in the living area. The poor woman's legs bore the splinters of unfinished wood that she demanded her kids assist with removing from the areas beyond her reach.

In those days, no one ever questioned why a woman would be in many different stages of black and blue. It was an unwritten rule that a wife was a husband's property and he was entitled to whatever fruits and benefits that could be reaped or raped from her. Pa would rant and rave in French, pound upon Ma, and then pass out either in his chair or bed or whatever happened to be within falling distance. No one ever asked questions, and no one ever discussed it. It was just the way it was.

Chapter 5

BLOOD BY MORNING

Time moved forward much like a mule hooked up to a plow. Sometimes the days dragged on for Beatrice, and at other times, the extensiveness of her chores would make her more determined to get to the end of the day, to the magical finish line—a place that never actually existed. She just made a U-turn and began all over again, day after day.

Beatrice loved her mother with a combination of pity, sadness, and adolescent admiration even though her ma never paid her much mind, unless of course she was a basket short or late in returning home. Even when Beatrice's sisters were cruel to her, which was more often than not, Ma looked away, not wanting to be bothered. Predictable like a tornado was everyday life for Beatrice.

It was a blessing that neither Beatrice nor her siblings ever received the honorary beating that was so common in her home. Pa would tie on a good one and then threaten them all that there would be "blood by morning."

Beatrice never quite knew what that meant exactly but lost many nights of sleep wondering if everyone would still be in one piece in the morning.

"Blood by morning" became the household motto. A phrase like that needed little clarification. Somebody would suffer; that was clear. She waited for it like a child waits for the tooth fairy, but this visitor wouldn't be bringing pennies.

A. Tacked

Most nights, Beatrice lay in bed with her forefingers pressed tightly into her ears, plugging and muffling out the hollow sound that fists hitting flesh made from the beatings her mother was receiving in the adjacent room.

Eventually, the room would grow silent except for the deep rumbling of pa's snoring.

Beatrice would finally drift off into sleep and into the dream, the same dream that she had had for as long as she could remember—a dream so pleasantly disturbing that others would think her mad if she ever dared tell it to anyone, a dream that could only come from the deepest and darkest places of one's mind, maybe from a mind that had seen more pain and fear than most, perhaps a mind that had been wounded one too many times.

Before her, a bath of warm, red blood was waiting. As Beatrice looked down into the tub, her eyes caught the playful, shimmering motion of the light from the overhead as it caught the sheen off the bathwater. A brilliant pattern of reflective light was cast throughout the tiny bathroom, as if the room were made of diamonds. Removing her clothes, Beatrice was overcome with desire. The silkiness of the blood felt good on her legs as she entered the tub and slid down deeper and deeper until the blood covered her head, leaving no trace of the Beatrice that was, the Beatrice now gone forever.

The ending was always the same. Death was very peaceful, a longing, a comfort until the consciousness took over and the dream was over for yet another night.

Beatrice knew there would be no room for siblings in death. The dream had comforted her in ways her brothers and sisters never could. It was time to pull away from those in her life. It wouldn't be too difficult. The tub was meant for her, and she would not share it with anyone. There would be no hand-me-downs on the other side. There would be no room for regret; the dream was meant for her and her alone. Once the decision had been made, Beatrice felt reborn. She would keep her head down, pick her berries, and wait. She would be prepared; she would be ready. Death would not be something to fear; it would be life's reward after a long, long day.

Chapter 6

BOARDING THE TRAIN

Free at last, Clayton thought as his mother, Linda, signed her name to the military enlistment papers. "Legal guardian, permission required," the paperwork read. The word *guardian* brought a chuckle to Clayton. Linda was a lot of things, a whole host of four-letter adjectives came to mind.

Guardian would be a new one; he hadn't heard of that one until then.

It had been a hard sell for the paper-pushing recruiter man. But in the end, his stupid grin, which creased from ear to ear, and his ridiculous flirting with Clayton's mother had paid off. The armed forces were going to make a man out of Clayton.

Clayton had barely cleared his seventeenth birthday, which like each and every birthday before, had gone completely unnoticed. He had been pitching hay into the stalls when one of his uncles who had been visiting and his granddad made their way to the barn. Their conversation continued as Clayton strained to catch every word from the safety of the bales. There had been a plea on the radio for the American people to step forward and enlist. World War II had finally reached its end, but there was still a massive amount of cleanup and redirection that needed to go on, and the military was looking for eligible applicants to assist in their plans. Many of the soldiers and airmen had been transferred to Europe so there had been an immediate demand for local trainees to conduct drills and security on the home front. Security seemed right up Clayton's alley. After all, he had done a fine job of shooting all the strays that came nosing around the farm.

Hell, he could even sense exactly where Grandfather was within a hundred yards. An idea was beginning to take shape in Clayton's mind, and as Clayton heaved yet another forkful of hay, a plan of escape began to form, bringing a very rare smile to his face.

Clayton knew that even if he had dropped out of school shortly after the eighth grade—What the hell was a dumbass schoolteacher going to teach him that he couldn't teach himself out back with his twelve gauge?—there was no education requirement that would hold him back from the armed forces.

His only roadblock was the fact that he was still a minor and had to get written consent from a legal guardian. Free labor would be a hard thing for Granddad to give up. Clayton was hoping that pure hatred would win out over the chores that Clayton did on the farm. Fortunately for Clayton, hatred won out.

It could have been papers to Mars for all Clayton cared. A ticket to freedom and the hell away from the farm was good enough for him. As the ink was drying on the forms, Clayton was already gone in his thoughts. At seventeen years old, he had his whole life ahead of him. *No more taking shit*, he thought.

Compliments of Uncle Sam, a train ticket was placed in Clayton's hand and the clock was ticking. There was no packing that needed to be done.

The last and only other set of britches and flannels had worn themselves down to threads and probably wouldn't last another wear anyway. The only thing that worried Clayton was what to do with his only friend, his twelve-gauge shotgun. It seemed funny to Clayton that here he was, going to fight for his country or at least shoot the shit out of somebody or someone, and his one companion, Mr. twelve-gauge had to stay at the farm. *Half-cocked and ready*, he thought as he loaded his gun. Maybe a little surprise to leave in the barn. Carefully, Clayton caressed the barrel and nodded a good-bye as he laid his buddy sideways in the corner of the barn nearest the milking cans.

Chapter 7

ON THE HIGH ROAD

The train ride coursed on as Clayton, tucked under a faded work cap, caught a few minutes of sleep. It had been a long haul from the top of the map all the way to San Antonio, Texas. A few days on the tracks had invigorated him, and his spirits were at an all-time high.

Basic training would start once he got bunked in. Somewhere in the stack of paperwork they had expected him to read, it stated how long he would actually be in basic before he would be sent out to his duty station.

He felt a touch of gratitude to his usually nonexistent mother for carefully reading and signing each form, less she make a mistake and Clayton remain on the farm. Page after page of forms had been carefully filled out. Clayton hated the sound of rustling paper, and he was grateful that his mother had finally come in handy for something. The only words Clayton could remember from the mound of senseless papers was "becoming a man and being issued a gun, a new friend of cold and steel."

Clayton was finally going to be on the high road and in charge—or so it seemed to a boy already so tragically lost.

As the train made its way into the station and the pull of the brakes subsided, Clayton got a good, hard look at the man on the platform, waiting for him as well as the dozens of young recruits who had been in the passenger car traveling south with him. A man, at least a good foot taller than most, with shoulders bulked up like he had been swinging an ax for most of his life greeted the recruits with a bellowing, "Line up! Get out! Get down! Line up! I won't repeat myself. Grab your gear and get your asses in the bus!"

What the hell was this? Clayton thought as he made a quick, temporary decision to save any lip until he was sure he wouldn't have to head back to the farm before the night was out.

The TI, otherwise known as "Training Instructor Stone, Sir," nipped at the heels of the newbies, eager to make them toe the line and beat it into their heads who was in charge here. Without any doubt or hesitation, he let the intimidated group of pansies know that he already had their balls in a fist grip, and unless they wanted to become ladies, they had better show some respect. Clayton thought it was comical that the men were being called pansies. That was until it sank in that he was being called one as well.

It was a long bus ride to Lackland Air Force Base. The blood that pooled in Clayton's forehead from the bottled-up rage had given him a massive headache. He had been tricked into this shit, he thought. This was no ticket to freedom but just another form of hell, another kind of farm with just another old son of a bitch to drag him down. Clayton didn't know what was in store for him, but he felt certain that whatever shit he got, he would find a way to give it back at least tenfold. Suffering was going to be someone else's responsibility and burden from then on.

Clayton waited in the long line that issued his fatigues, blues, boots, hats, belts, and underwear. He hadn't owned this much clothing before. He wasn't sure who looked more like queers, the ones behind him being handed their issued monkey gear or the ones already wearing it. One thing was for certain, he was going to be the one to decide how long he would let them dress him up like they owned him.

After a couple more hours of shots, rules, regulations, housekeeping requirements, and verbal abuse, bunkees were paired up. Clayton braced himself for the worst. He had decided a long time ago who the keepers were and who the disposables were. Blonds were either queers or tramps, depending on which way they wagged; niggers were filthy animals; and anyone with red hair should have his or her throat cut. There was little room for tolerance, and it was just that kind of tolerance by all the others that caused the whole frigging world to go to hell, he thought.

With fifty-five men in a flight, they would be assigned to an open-bay dormitory. Clayton had overheard "big mouth, Training Instructor Stone, sir," say that they would be making a squadron from all new recruits because there were at least two flights of trainees. A lot of people to piss him off, he thought.

It seemed like someone had been looking out for him, as the bottom bunk was assigned to a good egg with a real man's brown brush cut. As the trainees tucked into their bunks for the night and prepared themselves mentally for the next eight weeks of physical and mental exhaustion, Clayton too was planning out his own survival plan.

Chapter 8

HOOAH

Days marched forward, and 0430 came early to most. Clayton was used to getting up before the roosters because the farm had demanded it. Final morning call at 0500 began the first formation of the day with shoes shined and shirts tucked. Clayton fell in line with the other fools. The workouts actually felt good to him—even though it was silly to Clayton to have to do push-ups, sit-ups, and drills all day with nothing to show for it. He did notice, however, that his biceps were filling out, and if nothing else, he felt stronger than most of the men. "Canaries," he chided them when the drill sergeants weren't in listening distance. He didn't care that most of the guys stayed away from him. They called him an asshole, and it felt pretty good that they didn't trust him. Maybe they weren't so dumb after all. Clayton kept his distance as well and played the game just as well as anyone.

Since basic training was only a couple of weeks away from completion, the drill sergeant half-approved and half-looked the other way, granting a night off from the base. "Let off a little steam, get back here by 2300, and don't cause any fights."

Clayton hadn't had his first taste of liquor yet since Granddad hadn't been much of a drinker, so he was looking forward to this chance.

The local bar was full of fresh-faced military boys, including Clayton and his squadron. With little money in the pocket of his government-issued pants, Clayton had to figure out a way to score some libations. As he watched, he noticed the boys had flocked around a couple of pool tables, acting like bees circling a hive. He noticed that they were betting for drinks, and the loser would buy. There wasn't room in Clayton's budget for losing, nor was there any way he would lose out to the likes of them either. It didn't take much persuasion to join the game—no more than a poke in the chest and an offhand threat to entitle Clayton to the next spot from whichever man lost. No one wanted any trouble, at least no one but Clayton.

Winning felt good to Clayton as he belted down his fourth brandy with a beer chaser. His head was spinning, but his thoughts had never been clearer.

It felt good to let loose, to relax and let the alcohol warm his insides.

Drinking gave him a chance to feel, something he hadn't done since that damn dog, Pal.

Reveille came calling at 0430, finding Clayton with a bitch of a hangover.

Clayton shook it off. "A man's headache," he could take it. It was a small price to pay for being king last night. He grabbed his shoes and headed out into the morning air for a mandatory run. A five-mile run to clear their heads. No doubt someone had been talking. Time was ticking, and as Clayton ran through the early morning hours, he counted down the days out of the Texas heat.

With the couple hours the men found free most nights, once they had gotten used to the exhaustion and demands from the all-day drills, they would disperse into informal activities. A couple of groups played cards, some checkers, and others slap boxing. No one could afford gloves to go around, so street boxing took on a tamer form of slap boxing. The men had been warned that if it got more physical than a couple of bruises, they would be disciplined, substantially.

Clayton was strong, and he knew it. The adrenaline that was coursing through his veins had amped up his ability to knock a man to his ass with an open hand. With an upward twist of a man's wrist, Clayton could send any poor bastard to his knees, simultaneously delivering an open palm to the bottom of his nose, all in a matter of seconds and all within a fraction of an inch from completely destroying every bone in his nose. "Most damage with the least proof," Clayton would instruct. He could hit with his right and help the guy up with his left hand, all the while nodding and making the other guy agree with him, "It feels good to be a man."

Clayton liked to refer to himself as "Billy the Kid," when he was administering his beatings. He would brag that he could do with his hands what Billy could do with his rifle. When and if he decided to finish up with their beating, they wouldn't know what hit them.

When the matches got out of hand, which was more often than not, Clayton tried to make sure he left the boxing matches with no hard feelings. He would promise drinks all around on the next weekend pass and would administer a couple of friendly and firm one-armed headlocks to show his pals that he was serious about his offers, all of them. Ironically, no one ever took their concerns about boxing up with the staff sergeant. Most just looked the other way or stayed as far away from Clayton as they could.

Hitting these men gave him a rush that was almost as good as a drink.

Clayton was a smart man, and he knew that he had to find ways to continue to feed his budding need to be in control at all costs and at all times.

It looked like the armed forces were getting better and better. They offered a lot more opportunity than he had originally expected. Not only was Clayton getting three squares a day and a bed that didn't have hay in it but also punching bags made out of leather as well as his new favorite, human hide.

Chapter 9

MONTANA BOUND

Graduation meant nothing much for Clayton. While all the other men hugged and kissed on their family members who had come down for the ceremony and chowed down on the refreshments some local women's chapter had laid out for them, Clayton clutched his duffel bag and swore off the foul mood that was clouding his head. Had he actually been stupid enough to think he would recognize anyone sitting out on the metal chairs that lined the backside of the dormitory? No one gave a shit about him, and he felt the same about the whole damn bunch of them. Sneering, he said under his breath, "You're either for me or against me." It didn't take much thought to know where he stood with that answer.

Clayton's first duty station would be in Montana. The brand-new base in Great Falls would be his new home. He was looking forward to the cooler weather and was ready to see something other than the flat, barren fields of Texas. He had missed the mountains and lakes from up north. Montana was going to be the place for Clayton, a place to start over, maybe even stay awhile. It seemed pretty sorry that he was now in the air force, but he was still taking a damn bus all the way to Montana.

The next leg of his military career was just starting. Up until then, it had just been a lot of taking orders and exercise. Now Clayton would have the chance to work toward something that would make him feel important. It hadn't been easy trying to control the rage that he carried with him during drill after drill. Clayton had nearly ground down his back molars from clenching his jaws and gritting his teeth. He had found something that numbed all of the bad emotions, but he couldn't sneak alcohol onto the base.

What would carry him now was the fact that he would soon be issued his own gun. In basic, he had to sign a damn gun out just to do drills.

Pretending to accidentally forget to check it back in one afternoon had cost him a hundred push-ups and a verbal ball twisting in front of the other men for being "a stupid-ass screwup," according to hot shit TI Stone, sir. Now Clayton was officially in the air force and part of his next assignment came with a gun—lock, stock, and barrel. He had missed his firearm dearly.

As soon as Clayton's feet hit the tarmac, his new sergeant was there to greet him and welcome his sorry ass to Montana. It took all of about five seconds to size this guy up. Sergeant Roberts was a prick—a redheaded prick with an attitude. His fat bulldog-like neck vibrated each time he raised his voice, which was just about every time he opened his mouth. Clayton's future was now in his new sergeant's hands.

He had hated Stone, but at least Stone hadn't looked like a pussy. Every time Roberts walked by or came anywhere near Clayton, a knee-jerk reaction would cause Clayton's hand to come up, ready to cuff the fat-ass. Clayton looked like a man intent on asking a question.

Little did anyone know his hand would have loved to palm-smash that fucker in the nose. Clayton's lips felt dry, his new situation made him feel shaky and on edge. Maybe a drink would settle the nerves. A little alcohol could go a long way in helping tame his foul mood. It was a damn shame that he couldn't get his hands on anything other than a frigging soda or a swallow of water. He had to keep himself under control; he couldn't risk nailing this bastard. *Maybe another day*, he thought. Each one of these pansies would jump at the chance to be a witness, kicking Clayton out on his ass. Their time was coming too. They were either for him or against him.

Chapter 10

UNRAVELING

The weeks dragged on while the men were adjusting to their new life in Montana. Clayton knew that a short furlough was scheduled for the Friday following the next round of duty-roster changes. The men were specializing, signing up, and conditioning for whatever division they thought they wanted to work in and be trained for during their military stint. Some were leaning toward technology, others toward communications, and still others toward flight and mechanics. A night out to celebrate was on the schedule.

Clayton was pumped up, ready for a little downtime filled by pool and a lot of drinking. After all, he had earned it. He had suffered long enough and had kept his mouth shut for a whole lot longer than he had imagined he could. *Well done, Airman*, he thought.

The shack that they called the Service Man Hideaway was large enough to hold three pool tables, a jukebox, and about twenty bar stools. It looked like the bar had been an afterthought—a should-they-tear-the-shed-down-or-keep-it kind of afterthought. Lucky for Clayton, it was hooked up with Bud on tap and some whiskey bottles that were calling his name. Brandy was his baby, but in a pinch, rubbing alcohol would have worked the same, he thought as he belted down his third shot.

The pool tables were running hot and cold for him. The damn balls seemed to have a mind of their own. Clayton knew that it only took one shitty player to ruin the run of the table for everyone else. He would be God-damned if it would be him.

Liquored up, Clayton wanted to dance but not to the tunes on the rusted-out jukebox. He was burning inside for a fight. Usually the whisky would act like a salve on his fury, but tonight, he felt like ripping the Band-Aid off.

Clayton knew that if he was to get his wish, he had to be fast and sneaky.

Drunk or not, he still remembered that he had a government bunk, clothing, a little jingle in his pockets, and three square meals a day compliments of Uncle Sam. *Maybe a couple more shots to calm the nerves*, he thought as he paid for one and picked up the shot still sitting by an elbow to his right.

Dumb son of a bitch next to him didn't notice his full shot glass. The Service Man was crowded, too crowded. Clayton laughed as he pictured the fire marshal being a drunk, tucked somewhere jammed between elbows and barstools.

Clayton was handsome and had a great sense of humor when he wanted to. Had he been able to make friends—if being human hadn't felt so awkward to him—Clayton might have been a real man's man. In his twisted world though, kindness was only a tool for him, a little bait. Like a dance between a spider and a fly, the results were the same. One would be the winner, and the other one would be the loser. Clayton demanded complete control in every situation, and he wouldn't accept anything less.

Clayton knew he would have better luck finding a fight outside the crowded bar—and fewer witnesses to rat him out in the morning. As Clayton found the front door, he noticed that with a hard push, he could hit a couple of servicemen who happened to be standing directly on the other side.

"Bonus points." He chuckled to himself. Surely, they would forgive a drunken fellow comrade. Clayton was quick to apologize with a shitty grin that didn't go unnoticed.

Clayton stumbled his way out into the parking lot, hoping there would be someone waiting out there for a fight. As he contemplated which end of the lot to look in first, he noticed fat-ass Sergeant Peckerhead Roberts, sir, approaching him. His fat neck was bouncing up and down to the beat of his own steps. Clayton couldn't resist the temptation to mock him and started shaking his own throat with his hands, yelling slurs and insults at his commanding officer. It didn't matter to Clayton that the sergeant was only approaching Clayton as he suspected that Clayton had had more than his share of alcohol. Clayton didn't need any provocation or reason; without any thought or hesitation, his right hand came up in a half salute and clocked the officer before he could open his mouth to reprimand him.

Roberts hit the ground at about the same time Clayton felt the cold steel bracelets connecting his wrists together behind his back. Compliments of the MPs who were doing security sweeps that night. Clayton had picked the wrong time to express himself. These witnesses weren't drunk, and they carried a badge and a gun. Clayton was screwed, and he knew it.

Chapter 11

DEAD ON ARRIVAL

The stockade came with its own charm, comprised of a rusty slop bucket for personal needs, two bunk rolls—bedbugs included—and a tiny broken sink.

Home sweet home for the next thirty days, the lease said. Clayton's hangover was the mother of all hangovers, like a bad toothache hitting him right between the eyes. Sleep hadn't come soon enough. Just as his need for sleep had finally won out over pain, he was awakened by an early morning arrival just a few feet away. "Shut up, you bitch in a box!" Clayton threatened the foul-smelling intruder.

The cell reeked of vomit as Clayton's new cellmate looked up at him from the slop bucket he was hugging between his arms and knees.

Fortunately, the military police let "Queer Eyes"—Clayton's nickname for the new arrival—out of the tank long enough to take a shower and wash off the putrid smell that had already managed to permeate the entire jail block. Clayton knew it was only because the MPs didn't want to have to breathe in the stench any longer. It didn't matter to Clayton what the reason was; he was quite relieved.

Time worked its way down the calendar as best as it could between concrete and steel. After a few intense moments, Clayton had convinced his new roommate with a little physical persuasion that if he kept his mouth shut and only spoke when Clayton told him to, he wouldn't kill him in his sleep. Clayton would do his best to keep his end of the deal as long as he felt a need to. Curiosity had been nagging in the back of Clayton's mind, so one morning after chow trays were picked up, he gave permission for Queer Eyes to speak. Clayton wanted to hear exactly how it was that he had ended up in the Clink Hotel in the first place.

Queer Eyes was all too happy to accommodate him and hoped that Clayton would decide that he was a real man and stop calling him names. As it went, after a couple of hours of quarter games, on a bet, he had emptied a beer and told the fellows that he had no use for the bottle so he was going to throw it through the back windshield of the lieutenant's four-door parked out back. His buddies had laughed at him and told him he didn't have the balls for it. So before he knew it, he had thrown the bottle clear through the back window, smashing out the glass. The noise had alerted a couple of company men out parking their cars, and they had cuffed him and dragged him off to jail.

Clayton didn't like giving compliments. After all, no one would have given him one, but he had to give Queer Eyes credit for having the balls to stir up some shit. He wouldn't tell him that. Why bother? "You are a stupid ass, Queer Eyes, and we are done talking." Disinterested and with a wave of his hand, Clayton dismissed Queer Eyes from further conversations.

Time was poking at Clayton, and his nerves were raw. There was no alcohol served in jail. This thought played over and over in Clayton's mind.

He had taken up smoking whenever he could threaten a smoke out of someone, but it wasn't the same. The high was short, and there was no adrenaline rush either. Queer Eyes must have sensed that Clayton was a ticking time bomb because he did his best not to make any sounds or move around much in the cell. Clayton was like a land mine waiting to go off—wanting to go off.

The military cops assigned to the clink knew that Clayton's time was almost over. Twenty-eight days served and two more to go. They had known that Clayton was a loose cannon. They had watched him size up every square inch of his holding cell, staring, waiting, while he clenched his teeth and jaws over and over again. They were glad that he wouldn't be their problem much longer.

Queer Eyes was feeling better. Soon he would recover his life again. He had suffered for his mistake and had sworn off drinking for the rest of his time on base. He had learned his lesson, and he would be damned if he would ever slip up again. His crazy cellmate would be a constant reminder of "drink and go to hell." Never again, he thought. One of his buddies from the bar the night that his world had fallen apart had felt sorry for him and had tried to help by dropping off some newspapers to cut the boredom and act as a distraction. As his time would be up in only hours and not days, a distraction was most welcome now.

The sound of pages rubbing against pages snapped Clayton out of his thoughts. He had drifted off into another world only to be yanked back by Queer Eyes' blatant disrespect for him. He had warned him what would happen if he didn't keep quiet. He had made it quite clear that there would be consequences if he pissed him off. Why should he warn him again? He had been very generous, and this was the thanks he was getting from Queer Eyes. Clayton could feel the tightness in his chest. Raw adrenaline was making his heart race. *Fight or flight*, he thought. He wouldn't back down; he didn't know how.

Clayton crossed the cell like a cat on the hunt. Queer Eyes hadn't time to do anything but look up into Clayton's eyes as Clayton covered his nose and mouth with both his hands. "No bruising this way, cleaner kill," Clayton said with a malicious smile. He looked into the pupils of Queer Eyes as they went from large and terrified to small and distant. "Night, night, canary, sleep well, okay?" Clayton could feel the man's life leave his body.

Clayton's hands felt electrified with power, and his body tingled. He placed the damn newspapers that had killed Queer Eyes open and across his face.

Queer Eyes looked like a man who had fallen asleep reading. Clayton's body felt hot, and his pulse raced. An incredible rush coursed through his veins. Queer Eyes had left him with a powerful souvenir of their time together, a gift that he would enjoy without hesitation. Looking down at the bulge pulsating behind his prison-issued pants, Clayton began to rub himself as he stared down at the lifeless body that in death had given him so much pleasure.

In the final countdown toward freedom, Airman John Brown was dead.

Chapter 12

AWARD OF DISHONORABLE DISCHARGE

Clayton knew that morning would bring freedom and passage back to his barracks with the other airmen. He had served his punishment, and soon he would be back on track. He had slept well through the night, and no one had taken notice yet of the stone-cold airman sheltered by last month's news. He hadn't understood it, but he had taken a definite liking to what his body could do when the circumstances were right. Boners were new to Clayton, and ejaculations were up there with a double shot and a chaser. Life was looking good and feeling even better.

He decided that it would be safer to act like he was still asleep when the guard passed through, offering his last cage-served breakfast. Sprawled out with his arms tucked behind his head, eyes closed, he listened to the guard attempting to rouse the lifeless body that lay a bunk away. Clayton was quick on his feet and a fast learner. He would act dumb and surprised just like the guard who was now raising his voice.

"On your feet, Airman, explain to me what happened to Brown!"

Clayton had to think quick, as now wouldn't be the time to refer to his dead cellmate as Queer Eyes. This commanding officer was new to Clayton. Maybe someone from the big-shot office, Clayton thought.

"I don't know, sir. You sure he's dead?" Clayton lowered his head and tried to appear sorrowful for a man that he only hours ago had drained the life out of. "I went to sleep in my bunk early last night around 2100 so I would be well rested for my dismissal today. Airman Brown here, sir, was reading when I last saw him."

The room became loud with the commotion of military police and officers Clayton hadn't seen before. He figured that if he acted dumb and humble, he would just ride the tide and soon, with no proof, he would be bunking in base. Poor sorry-ass Queer Eyes, he hummed to himself.

Later in the afternoon, long after Queer Eyes had been removed and transferred to the morgue, a familiar face stood outside the steel bars separating Clayton from his old life. He recognized the sorry son of a bitch Sergeant Roberts. Clayton knew that it was show time, and he had rehearsed this part in his head numerous times.

"I am really sorry that I hit you, sir. I got a little drunk and lost my head. I know that I belonged locked up for a while so I could sort out my priorities. I am really glad that I was able to pay my dues and look forward to working under your command again, sir."

Sergeant Roberts took his time, waiting out his own reply. He watched as Clayton shifted his body weight from one foot to the other. "Well, son, it's gonna be a short career for you. We don't have enough proof to lock your ass up until the next decade, not yet anyway, but we do have the power to boot your ass out of military service. Pack your bags, son. You are officially dishonorably discharged. Did you hear me? DD, dishonorable discharged. I worked hard to see that the paperwork would be ready in time to have you officially escorted off base. Good-bye, you sorry piece of shit! I wouldn't leave town just yet. Who knows who might come calling you with an arrest warrant?"

Clayton thought that he was interpreting the sergeant wrong. He had been so careful not to get tangled up, no proof, no evidence of a crime. How the hell was he getting pinned without proof? Clayton didn't like people speaking to him in that tone and certainly not the redheaded prick who stood in front of him, threatening him. Clayton's upper lip began to quiver. He needed revenge, and he needed it now. The military wasn't much, but it was his, and now it was being snatched out of his hands. Someone was going to pay, and Clayton knew exactly who that someone would be. He didn't need to go back to his bunk at the barracks. That life was over, and he didn't want any reminders of it. Soon after his last conversation with Roberts, two military police were escorting him to the other side of the locked gate. The military hadn't seen the last of him yet.

Chapter 13

ON THE RUN

Clayton had remembered where the owner of the Service Man tavern kept his car. Before he had gotten hammered last month, he had run into the guy from the other side of the bar. Seemed the old coot liked to keep a look out over his property and had built on a shed big enough for a twin bed and a small dresser. Living at the bar made his trip to work a hell of a lot easier, especially if he had enjoyed too much of his inventory the night before.

Clayton had liked the old-timer, but now he liked the car that was parked out back a whole lot more. Luckily for Clayton, no one locked their doors in 1948. No one had gotten particularly paranoid about break-ins and auto theft, at least not yet.

Clayton had barely enough money for gas so he was relieved when the gauge read a full tank. "Yes, the barkeep is a good old egg, sorry bastard," Clayton thought out loud. He knew that he had one more stop to make, and then he would be heading to the state line for good. He was glad that he had remembered to lift a couple of six-packs from the storage shed before he drove off in the stolen Fairlane.

Roberts would be leaving the base shortly past 1900 for his weekly poker game in town. He had been bragging about his poker skills ever since Clayton had arrived on base. It seemed like there was a dive about a couple miles outside of Great Falls, where a military sergeant or better could try out his luck with the cards and with the ladies who worked for profit on the side. Clayton would wait down the road and hope that Roberts's habit hadn't been altered by the day's excitement. Clayton was pumped up and had a good feeling about his plan. It would be worth watching Roberts bleed out when Clayton's fist connected with his nose. This time, Clayton wouldn't worry about proof or broken bones; there wouldn't be leniency.

Clayton pushed back a few of the beers while he waited for Roberts's car.

He had built up quite a thirst and appreciated the feel of the beer as he sucked down the last from one of the six-packs. Being pissed off was hard work, and he was ready for his payday. Fortunately, Roberts was the hound that Clayton thought he was. Like clockwork, the sergeant's car lights turned down the short road leading up to the building. "The cardsharp's home away from home." Clayton would only have a few minutes before someone would hear the commotion and come out with his service revolver in hand. Clayton had to work fast, yet linger long enough to enjoy the moment he had been dreaming about.

Roberts lumbered out of the seat of his old Buick and started tucking in his shirt, which had come out from the busting-at-the-seams service pants.

He didn't notice Clayton until it was too late. By the time he figured out his situation, he was already preoccupied, choking on the blood that was running through his sinus cavities. Clayton had put a solid hit with all the force of an angry, completely out-of-control man square in Roberts's nose. By Clayton's assessment and by the looks of things, the nose that once was there was now lodged behind the man's broken jawbone and stuck like glue to the back of his skull. Robert gagged on the blood and human tissue that was plugging his windpipe, his face unrecognizable. Clayton wanted to make sure that Robert remembered who took his life away so he held him by the back of the hair facing him until all of the life drained out of his eyes and they fell closed for good.

Clayton could feel the warmth of Roberts's blood on his face and hands.

It was a deed well done from his assessment. The only thing left was to see if old Roberts had anything special in his car to share with Clayton.

Clayton wanted something to remember him by, a souvenir of their time together or a trophy for his fine work. Fortunately for Clayton, a Krag rifle with bayonet holder still intact was tucked away under the backseat. It was the perfect trophy for the perfect kill.

Clayton knew that Roberts had been married. He had overheard him talking one day about his girl at home. Clayton had never cared anything about other people, but now he wished he had found out what her name was.

Well, he would have to give it a guess. Clayton looked down at the Krag and stroked its barrel gently. "It's time to go home now, Betsy. Trust me; you and I are going to have a good time together." Clayton would keep this gun as a reminder of his dance with the military. Roberts's death would always be the most special to him. Roberts had given him something that he had never had before, a taste of someone else's blood pouring warm and thick against him.

Chapter 14

US ROUTE 89

Clayton was making good time as he pulled out onto Highway 89. Time was on his side now, he thought as he rolled down the windows and twisted a cap from one of the remaining three beers. He played with the dial on the radio to see if there was anything he recognized. He wasn't much for singing, but tonight he would make an exception. Clayton needed to find a gas station with a toilet so he could finish wiping the blood from his face and hands. He felt like a warrior, and each time he looked into the rearview mirror, he saw looking back at him a man on top, a man in charge.

Clayton knew Highway 89 would take him out of Montana. From there, he would decide where he would travel to next. It had been a lucky break that payday had come the day before the bars had closed behind him. When he had cleaned out his pockets at lockup, it had been hard handing over the rolled-up cash money that added up to his entire life savings. He could imagine it being spent up in a good poker game between the sergeants and the lieutenants. It had come as a complete surprise that all of it was accounted for in the manila envelope of his personal belongings that was returned to him when he was released.

It was time for a stop, maybe a little pool and a few shots. With all the blood now freshly washed from his face, it was time to step into his new life. He knew that it would take at least a couple of days before the police would even start to put two and two together. Finding a dead sergeant would spark a full investigation. Fancy DNA testing hadn't been developed yet, luckily for Clayton. Even though the fresh mountain air of Montana had been calling, Clayton knew that he would be saying good-bye after that night.

Settling the score would be a fond memory he could always come back to in his head; moving on would give him the distance he needed from the authorities. "If they want to question me, let them come find me," he said to no one in particular.

The intense adrenaline rush from the kill had sucked all the moisture from Clayton's mouth. His throat felt parched, as if he had been swallowing handfuls of sand. He had earned a little downtime, and the Tin Roof Bar and Tavern had a good feel—not very loud, dim lighting, and the four or five cars parked out front meant that there wouldn't be a lot of drunken men to agitate him. He would kick back for a while and relive his splendid performance in the parking lot of Aces and Spades.

Clayton found a barstool front and center and went about his business of ordering a brandy with a beer chaser. The man on Clayton's left had heard his order to the barkeep and remarked that Clayton had good taste. Clayton was in a generous mood. After all, he had bagged some big game that night and he felt like celebrating. "Order one of the same for my buddy here."

The men clicked shot glasses and swallowed the brandy in one gulp.

After a couple more rounds, Clayton and his drinking buddy, Hank, started talking music. Clayton hadn't found many reasons to sing, but he could put words together in such a way that would make anyone take notice.

A man of many talents, Clayton thought to himself. It had a nice ring.

Hank and Clayton started talking about how the world was changing all around them. Life could be a struggle, and they both had come upon hard times over the years. Of course, it didn't matter that neither of them really had much experience with life. Hank was just a handful of years older than

Clayton and barely that. Clayton started saying in a raised voice, hooked to a country twang, that no matter how he struggled and strived, he was barely getting by. He showed Hank the work boots that he had managed to keep, compliments of the military. Those boots would have to last a while because they were the only thing between Clayton's feet and the dirt road. Clayton made silly tunes up for most of their conversation. Before long, the two men were teetering on their barstools, singing their homegrown version of what a man sounds like when he is fully tanked up.

Clayton liked Hank, as he could drink and he could rhyme his words like nobody's business. He hadn't met anyone that he could cut loose with and holler with without wondering what they would look like dead.

As the barkeep was cleaning up for the night, a liquored-up Hank and Clayton made their way to the front door. It had been a good time, and now it was time to get back on the road. Clayton shook Hank's hand, which wasn't something he did as a regular thing. "Hank Williams, you are a helluva guy and a good fella too. Hope we meet again."

Clayton stumbled to the old four-door, looking in the backseat of the car, making sure Betsy was still resting there. Fortunately, she was there to greet him on the backseat floorboard. Clayton slumped into the driver's seat and started the engine. "Head for the state line and take it from there," he slurred.

As the Ford's wheels hit the pavement and made a left onto the highway, Clayton laughed as he thought about his good old buddy Hank. They had truly hit the nail on the head on their last tune, for damn sure, he thought.

Tapping his index finger on the dashboard, Clayton belted out a line from their final song together, "I'll never get out of this world alive."

Part 2

BREAKING GROUND

I am dead. Only vengeance can restore me!
Only victory can return my life to me!
—Terry Goodkind

Chapter 15

BEATRICE BECOMES A WOMAN

Beatrice smoothed down the front of her pretty plaid skirt. She was proud that her time and talents behind a sewing machine had paid off. Ma had decided when Beatrice became sixteen that it was time to spend her day on more serious pursuits, so Beatrice had dropped out of school and became a full-time seamstress. The money was better than the change she made when she was a young girl picking berries in the fields. In those days, educating a female was low priority compared to any money she might be able to bring in to help support her family.

At first, she hadn't thought that she would ever learn to follow the lines on the tissue-paper patterns and cut the fabric out the way her mother demanded. With money too tight to even imagine ruining a yard or so of fabric, Beatrice learned that precision with the scissors and control of the old Singer would be crucial. When she wasn't sewing for her own family, she was working in town, making curtains, dresses, and skirts for those who could afford to pay for them. With more time spent away from the house, Beatrice could relax a bit and not be underfoot when Pa went off on his tirades. Even though time had taken away the remaining tuffs of Pa's hair, he continued to nurse his liquor bottle and drag Beatrice's ma across the floor. Fortunately, the old wooden floors that used to give Ma splinters had been replaced with linoleum when Beatrice's family had moved across town, following the death of her older brother in World War II. Overall, nightly entertainment had not changed much over the years, so Beatrice welcomed some time to herself.

Beatrice hadn't been all that interested in the opposite sex. She had seen what a big responsibility they could be, and she wasn't in any hurry to hook up with one, at least not yet. Had it been up to her, she probably would have settled for more quiet nights by herself over any night carousing with one of her older sisters. As it was not ladylike for young women to be seen alone in a bar in 1948, Beatrice's older sister used that to her advantage and persuaded Beatrice to pair up with her on a regular basis. A little quality sister time—and maybe some male company too—was the promise.

Beatrice was a fine looker, and the locals found her alluring. With a tapered, tight figure and large breasts, she managed to attract a lot of attention at the Corner Tavern. Silky black hair blanketed with pin curls cascaded down her face, and her perfectly painted red lips looked as if they longed to be kissed. Yes, Beatrice could turn heads. Her older sister had figured out that men usually traveled in pairs too, so she never felt left out. Beatrice never had the urge to try alcohol, although she had many men who offered to buy her some. She had figured that she would leave the drinking up to the men. "Let them make fools of themselves." Sadly, it never crossed her mind that there were men out there who didn't want or have to drink, actual men who didn't need to make fools of themselves. Ginger ale was her drink of choice when she visited the Corner Tavern. They always remembered to put it in a short glass so Beatrice would fit in. The barkeep knew it was the ladies who kept the men coming in to buy drinks. He didn't want someone like Beatrice to slip through his fingers by finding another place to spend her time.

Chapter 16

CLAYTON COMES TO TOWN

Clayton had spent a good part of three days on the tarmac. He looked edgy and worn down. He had made the decision on the second day that with what spending money was left in his pockets, his priorities would need to be gas, alcohol, and food—in that order. It had been a hard decision to make, coming back to the town that had caused him so much aggravation.

Clayton knew that there were plenty of logging camps that were always looking for a man who knew the woods and could swing an ax. He had to find a way to get some cash money, so living in the woods sounded pretty good to him.

Logging into Canada was big business. Even the exchange rate on the funny money they paid the loggers was worth it. Clayton knew that he would have to work hard to get even a small cut of that money. He had no truck so he would have to work for someone else. "Desperate times call for desperate measures," Clayton said to no one in particular. *The good thing about working in the woods is you don't have to make conversation with anyone,* he thought. Clayton knew that he could do the work. What better place to hide out than deep in the woods, toting an ax.

The man who signed Clayton on barely missed his shoes with the chewing tobacco juice he spat out onto the ground. Usually, a deliberate act of disrespect like that would have caused Clayton to be powerfully angry.

Instead, Clayton was amused to see this old son of a bitch chewing on a wad of tobacco like it was a ten-dollar steak. Clayton thought it wouldn't hurt to ask, so with his best manners and naturally manipulative way, he asked the old-timer for a chew. The man, surprised by Clayton's request, handed him a wad and made a comment that he would take it out of his pay on Friday.

Clayton couldn't tell if the old man was making conversation or was being an ass. Hell, Clayton didn't even know if he was going to make it until Friday anyway. "Appreciate it," Clayton mumbled and waved back as he packed his left cheek with the entire wad of tobacco.

Chewing tobacco took getting used to. You had to be careful not to swallow the juice, lest it come back up through your nose. It was pretty foul shit, but it had a quality that Clayton liked. No matter how long you kept it wedged in your check, it never gave up its flavor and it made it pretty damn impossible to carry on a conversation with anyone. Clayton decided that it was a lot easier to thrust an ax into a tree with both hands than one on an ax and one on a cigarette. He felt pretty good that life seemed to be more in his control now.

The logging camps were made up of a lot of odd men. Clayton seemed to fit right in. Most just wanted to tend to their own business and be left alone. Probably a good number had the authorities looking for them.

Working alongside these men suited Clayton fine, as no one made small talk. The work was hard, and the pay was decent. There were sandwiches laid out at the noon hour and some soup or stew set out for supper. Many of the stragglers lived at camp; they had no families to go home to. Others stayed the week and packed it out on the weekends to resume a normal life. Whatever their circumstances, there were at least a dozen or so at any given time swinging axes and making their mark in the forest. Home was under the stars, bedding down with the mosquitoes for Clayton. The creek ran alongside the patch of ground he had claimed as his own, so his weekly bathing needs were easily attended to. Clayton was a man on his own now.

He liked being his own boss and looked forward to the day he might take charge of someone else too. It was time for Clayton to look for a woman.

Chapter 17

IODINE AND MECURICOME

The Corner Tavern had been busy that Saturday night. The regulars were crowded around the pool table, and those on dates were jamming the jukebox with dimes. Beatrice and one of her older sisters were pretending to be interested as they gazed over to the pool table, waiting for the next round of players, "someone new to stare at."

Beatrice had found a handsome man back in the spring who had come over to share her supper table a time or two. LaRosa had asked Beatrice's pa if it would be okay to court his daughter, and Pa had given his blessings. Seemed that the old pickup had needed some work so perhaps they could figure out a nice trade for Beatrice's hand. Pa was always the entrepreneur, especially after an all-night workout with a six-pack of tall boys. Beatrice didn't want to be rushed into anything, and marriage hadn't looked all that great to her.

After all, how could she raise her own family when she was still paying off her room and board in the house she grew up in? But she had to admit, the dark-haired stranger with the irresistible chocolate-brown eyes had made her head turn. It was peculiar how he seemed to do all the right things for her.

He had opened the doors and had even stood up when she had entered a room. This behavior was a mystery to Beatrice, and she was afraid that he wasn't to be trusted. She had almost stopped herself a few weeks back when he had kissed her lips and neck in ways she had never experienced. One thing had led to another, and before long, Beatrice had found herself in the backseat of his car. He had said that he loved her, but Beatrice had gathered her clothes and run back home. She had to think about the future and protect herself from men she couldn't predict.

Beatrice spotted Iodine and Mecuricome seated in the laps of two military boys that they had sweet-talked over at the jukebox. Iodine and Mecuricome were the ugliest tramps this side of the Canadian border.

Fortunately for the both of them, they looked just fine in the dark and even better after a couple of shots. Every local knew those two would put out for the evening. A few unlucky ones had returned from a night of carousing with a gift they couldn't return, a bad case of the clap. No one had remembered what the girls' real names were. One man had received his gift and had come in the tavern with his balls on fire, ranting and hollering that he needed antiseptic just to be in the same room as them. Hence, the names Iodine and Mecuricome were born. Funny thing, the ladies thought that the nicknames were darling, and from time to time, you could hear one belt out the other's name across the tavern in a tone that resonated throughout the place as if they were calling in the hogs for dinner. Yes, they were quite the pair. It seemed most men were bent on taking their chances for a promised night of screwing. Like a gambler with a pocket of cash and a deck of cards, these fools decided they would play their odds and see what was to happen. A few of the regulars had even taken to working some side bets to see who the next sucker would be, lining their pockets with others' misfortunes.

No pain, no gain.

Beatrice was on her second ginger ale and was trying to think of a polite way to tell her sister that she was bored. She hadn't been interest in looking at other prospects since the romp in the backseat. Really all she wanted to do was to go home. As she was sorting out the words that would enable her exit, an attractive man with chestnut hair and azure eyes opened the door to the Corner Tavern. His muscles rippled as he swung the door open and let it fall back into its casing behind him. He looked rugged and charming. Beatrice had never seen him in the Corner Tavern before.

Clayton noticed this woman with the strikingly pretty dark eyes. She had a look that was pure, not like the tramps he had stumbled onto in the logging camps. He had called those whores opportunists, as they could hear the jingle of change in a man's pocket a mile away. This woman sitting on the bar stool wasn't one of those ladies. Her modest dress was long at the knee and high at the chest. This one wouldn't have expectations of Clayton and wouldn't know something was wrong if Clayton had any trouble getting himself up for the occasion.

Beatrice smiled her crooked smile, her signature smile, the smile that would find her face a thousand times during the course of her life.

Always the same words came to her mind when those lips would part, "I'm crazy like a fox." With a tilt of her head and that smile, she could say yes and say no all at the same time. She had perfected that crooked smile one night as she stood over Pa after he had passed out on the hall floor. It was the first time she had truly allowed herself to feel hatred for the man. The temptation of tripping onto his Adam's apple with the heel of her shoe was intoxicating.

As luck would have it, Pa rolled onto his side as if on cue, and the idea was laid to rest. It had tickled her so that she could feel those powerful feelings so intensely yet still be able to smile down on him like a caring daughter.

"Crazy like a fox, and dangerous behind those big, beautiful brown eyes."

Beatrice didn't know what to think of this stranger. His eyes were the color of ripening blueberries in cream. What harm would it do if she let him buy her a ginger ale? Clayton walked slowly to the empty seat next to Beatrice. He didn't want to seem eager and weak. As he hoisted himself onto the stool, he casually asked the barkeep for a double brandy and a beer and then as an afterthought, added, "And one of whatever the lady is having too." For the better part of an hour, both Clayton and Beatrice stared out into the crowded tavern, neither of them succumbing to small talk. Clayton was a man of few words. *The strong, silent type*, Beatrice thought.

Clayton hadn't spent much time around the opposite sex, but he knew they had something that he couldn't get from the crazy men he worked with. Clayton looked over at Beatrice and offered to give her a ride home.

Beatrice was flattered that this handsome man with the firm jaw was paying attention to her. Her time spent with chocolate eyes was pushed to the back of her mind. There was something Beatrice liked about this man of few words. There was something familiar and comfortable. Maybe she would find that they had something in common. "I'm not like them," Beatrice said while tipping her head in the direction of Iodine and Mecuricome.

Clayton laughed and helped Beatrice push her stool away from the bar. "I know; that is why I asked you."

Chapter 18

CODEPENDENTS

Beatrice hadn't minded that Clayton smelled often of pine pitch. The scent of perspiration and pitch had made Beatrice want him even more.

Time seemed to fly when Clayton and Beatrice were together. As the season passed, Beatrice's oldest sister had gotten married and was no longer a regular at the Corner Tavern. With each passing day, LaRosa and the memories of the backseat of his car began to fade away for Beatrice.

Clayton continued to drink, but Beatrice was accustomed to men with bottles, and it didn't worry her much when Clayton would drink and pass out.

Clayton was on top of the world, riding high. Unbeknownst to him, that would be a short trip. Work was still steady and lucrative in the logging camp. With the passing weeks, men left and others came to take their place.

Room and board was still provided by the dense trees, running streams, and daily dinner bells. Clayton liked the fact that there were no walls between him and the outdoors. As long as Beatrice continued to make no demands on him, he would keep her around. He had her for sex and whatever else he might need her for. Beatrice's ma hadn't liked Clayton much, but he had forgiven her, as her reason was plain and simple— Clayton was just too handsome for Beatrice. Clayton couldn't fault her for that; after all, he was.

What money he had left after his weekly expenses payable to Corner Tavern and the local goods and supply store was carefully buried under a heap of pine needles and a couple flat stones. Clayton's type of banking could be done at all hours of the day, including weekends, without a service fee. A couple of times, after pushing back a few, he had hinted around to the canaries he worked with, stirring up some curiosity on where they might find some "pay dirt." Clayton hadn't had any real action since Montana, so anything he could do to stir up any kind of trouble, he felt obliged to do. "A man has to make his own kind of entertainment," Clayton liked to say.

The North Country was known for its short spells of good weather and its painfully long winter chill. As the fall temperatures started to decline and the changing winds kicked up a flurry of leaves, Clayton knew that logging would come to a screeching halt for the season shortly after the first snowfall, which usually was measured in feet and not inches. By the look of things, he knew that winter weather was pushing at the calendar faster than he had expected. Planning had never come easily for Clayton, especially when it went against the grain of what he wanted to do when he wanted to do it. God had a way of pulling the rug out from underneath him and Clayton didn't appreciate anyone laughing at him. God was no exception.

He shook his fist up toward the heavens as the wind blew and the temperature plummeted down into the thirties about a month sooner than expected. "Someday, you and I are going to have a go at it," he threatened his maker.

Beatrice had been all too happy to oblige when Clayton had offered to let her come work alongside him at the camp. "Being in the fresh air would be good for you," Clayton had suggested. With the cooler weather, it would help to have two sets of hands pulling in a paycheck. The camp didn't let women sign on as labor, but they didn't argue when Clayton assured them that Beatrice just wanted to be near her man. "You know, the jealous type."

Beatrice did her best to haul the trees down the skid way, keeping up with Clayton. Maybe if she kept her end of the bargain, Clayton would keep his promise to marry her in the spring. Beatrice had always been taught that she had to earn her keep, and this was to be no different.

Beatrice had grown tired of fabric and thread long before she had found herself pitching wood hooks into hardwood trees. She had hoped that the feeling of fatigue that had come over her the last couple of weeks was just a passing thing and the outdoors would help to get her back on her feet.

Mornings were starting out more regularly with dry heaves knee down into Clayton's washbasin she knew as the creek. She had to be careful not to let Clayton see her weak and lame. After all, he might not want her. The egg sandwiches served at lunchtime hadn't helped much with settling her stomach. Beatrice had remembered watching the same progression with her mother. The end result had been a younger sister. What would Clayton say when he found out? How long would it be before she would have to tell him?

Chapter 19

MARRIAGE BY DEFAULT

Clayton had wanted to kill her the night that Beatrice shared her awful secrets with him. She had sneaked up on him after a couple of shots of brandy and revealed the bad news to him with such zest that he had thought she had won something. In 1950, there was no such thing as having a baby out of wedlock. It just wasn't done. Shotgun weddings were the order of business anytime the order of things got turned around. There were just some things a man shouldn't look away from. Clayton would be chained to his previous bribe of marriage by spring with the exception that it came six months early and saddled to a newborn.

Clayton's high road had just gotten gullied out by bad weather.

Beatrice's words had stuck to the back of his throat like a bad case of thrush, and the alcohol wasn't cutting the sting. Clayton was in a foul mood. Had Beatrice been a few siblings shy, had she not been seen around camp, she might have simply just disappeared, left town. Just a few stones shy of a "never after." Too many people would be asking too many questions, and Clayton didn't like being sloppy. The notion of being a father set his jaws to aching as he ground down the last of his rear molars, "just a cruel fucking joke." There had to be something in it for him? A soon-to-be wife and a baby due in March. Clayton had dangled the marriage carrot in front of Beatrice to keep her working and keep the sex coming. Here he was now shackled to his new set of unfortunate events. What the hell had happened?

Even if he could persuade the foreman from the logging camp to let Beatrice move down in the clearing with him, there would be no way anyone would allow him to spend the winter tented up with a pregnant wife—even if he didn't care if she froze to death or not.

***

The wedding ceremony conducted in the front room of Beatrice's parents' house lasted all of about five minutes, which was about four and a half minutes longer than Clayton wanted to stand up and look happy in front of the preacher man. Fortunately, Beatrice's father believed in celebrating any circumstances and wasn't selfish with the liquor he was pouring to commemorate the day's events.

Beatrice's mother helped put the last of Beatrice's clothes into the satchel she had given her as a wedding present. It seemed like it was as good a time as any to get the "wifely duty" talk out of the way. Beatrice was no stranger to the goings-on in the bedroom. Her hard, swelling belly was proof enough of that. She had heard some of the standard advice that Ma had given her other sisters, as each of them took their vows of matrimony. This time wouldn't be any different, except she wouldn't be the one listening in from the other side of the door.

"Marriage is a duty and a privilege. Don't let your man want for anything. Fix your hair up nice for him and let him dress you up feminine, in ruffles and dresses. Make sure you ask for his opinion often, as it is really the only one that matters. Be rosy and loving and work hard. Don't ever deny your husband sex; you don't get to say no, ever. Remember to always take your beatings as a good wife should."

Beatrice hauled her satchel out with one arm, stammering under her breath the powerful words her mother had just said. Her other arm was wrapped tightly as support around her intoxicated new husband.

"One more thing," her words echoed behind as Beatrice struggled to release her responsibilities into the old rusted-out four-door. "Don't ever try to come back home; you're married now. Your bed is not here anymore. You made your bed; now you go lie in it."

It was hard to tell which clouds were getting darker, the ones in the sky or the ones coming together in Beatrice's head. "Crazy as a Fox," had a new set of responsibilities, like it or not.

Chapter 20

THE FOUR-ALARM TENEMENT HOUSE

"A real fixer-upper," Mr. Nobody said for the second time. Clayton leaned back on his barstool, thinking all the while that advice and chitchat always seem to go hand and hand with a free drink. Clayton never lost at the pool table so he had his share of no-cost alcohol. He was in a good mood, though, and was enjoying his time at the Corner Tavern. His new bride had come dangerously close to a backhander from all of her bitching about living in the old canvass tent. Maybe he should just bury her under it and see how that worked for her. What a stupid, dangerous thing for her to do. Three days married and she still hadn't figured out her place yet. Clayton would be a good teacher, when the time was right.

Some of Mr. Nobody's blather had paid off. The two-story tenement house, a couple miles outside of town, had been left and abandoned by its original owner. A new owner had paid the property tax up and had wanted to work the farmland behind it but didn't have much use for the house.

Luckily for Clayton, all it took was two months' rent at a decent price and the newlyweds could move in immediately. Hell, Clayton had two months of rent money in his personal bank of dirt and pine. Beatrice would owe him for this find and owe him good.

Moving was a simple task. Other than the borrowed tent and a handful of personal items, moving was just basically getting in the car and driving to the house. Clayton had recently stumbled upon an old hunting dog by the creek that had followed him around, no place to go. He had been calling the old dog Rinney, named after the drifter who had strayed into camp during the summer months. This old drunk had sealed his fate by passing out under a falling tree, operative word being *falling* and not fallen. The old coot didn't know what had hit him. Rinney seemed like just as good a name as any for a dog, Clayton had thought. The damn dog had legs so short it looked like it was crawling on the ground. It was comical watching the stupid creature struggling to get its hindquarters up off the ground and into the car.

After about the second or third try, old Rinney managed to get into the backseat and off Clayton's family went.

The fixer-upper hadn't seen a paintbrush in some time. The front door stuck, and the steps had caved in probably at the turn of the century. The inside wasn't much better. Between the peeling wallpaper, cobweb-cloaked windows, and rotting wooden floors, the place just looked damn creepy. Beatrice started wondering if the canvas tent by the creek was really that bad after all. She knew that it would be her job to make the house into a home no matter how much elbow grease it took. Clayton had done his job of providing for her, and now the rest was up to her. Fixing up the place to make it livable was women's work.

The upstairs was more room than the both of them needed, even with the baby on the way. Beatrice had gone up there the day they moved in just out of curiosity and hadn't wanted to return. It looked like there had been a bedroom or two up there, but time and neglect had made it look more like an abandoned attic. Beatrice found no reason to tend to it now. She had more pressing tasks at hand. Her days spent in the house were busy cleaning, mopping, and clearing away stray spiders and wasp nests. Beatrice was determined to make the four walls her four walls.

Not long after moving in, Clayton and Beatrice started hearing the stairs leading to the second floor creaking throughout the night. It sounded like someone with heavy boots was making his way to the top of the landing only to come back down again, slow and steady. Most nights, this would happen three or four times. Rinney couldn't be blamed, as he couldn't manage the stairs and took to howling as he looked up the staircase night after night into whatever invisible thing was causing all of the commotion.

To Beatrice's relief, daylight hours were peaceful. The house seemed to settle down, and other than an occasional creak from the floorboards, all was still. Come nighttime though, it was altogether a different story. It was becoming quite clear that someone or something else had set up housekeeping alongside Beatrice and Clayton. As if the sound of footsteps wasn't enough to set the hair on the back of the neck on edge, the nighttime visitor invented a more persuasive way to get its housemates' attention. The first time Beatrice heard the roar and the crackling of burning papers upstairs, she nearly screamed. Clayton had long passed out, his solution to the noisy late nights. Fearing for her own life, Beatrice had run up the stairs with a howling Rinney looking up, terrified at the unseen instigator whose presence he could only sense. Beatrice was stunned when she reached the second floor and nothing was on fire, nor had anything been disturbed. There were no papers on the floor or anywhere else. According to the conditions right in front of her, the roar as loud as a freight train and the rustle of burning papers never existed and couldn't have happened.

Frazzled from lack of sleep, a growing baby inside of her, and a husband more pickled than last year's pears, Beatrice grew anxious and more afraid.

Night after night, the torment continued. On one particular evening, the roar of the invisible fire came with a vengeance. The flames could be heard licking at the wallpaper from the upstairs rooms. The downstairs lit up with the glow of red and yellow-orange shadows. Clayton could even smell the smoke so strongly that it burned his nose. Enough was enough, the fire had to be there; it was too real for it not to be. Clayton grabbed his Krag and headed upstairs, swearing the whole way. He was bound and determined to put this frigging nightmare to rest. Clayton returned, walking slowly until he finished on the last step. "Get your coat, grab a few clothes, and get your ass in the car."

A. Tacked

By the look on Clayton's face, Beatrice didn't have to ask. There hadn't been a fire that night or any other night for that matter. Something wanted them to leave, and by damn, they were going to do just that. As Clayton slammed the door behind them, Beatrice could have sworn she saw something dark and ominous out of the corner of her eye.

Chapter 21

FIRSTBORN

We are not in Kansas anymore. By the way, Glenda the good witch,
she won't be coming back, at least not in your lifetime. In fact, I
think she was the one looking up, hollering, "Oh no!" when the
house landed on top of her. Oh, yeah, the flying monkeys? Well, they
are real too. You will see them later, but they will look just a little
bit differently than you might expect. Nighty, night, my baby.
—bedtime story

Beatrice was having a difficult time shaking off her memories of the four-
alarm house. Maybe the black shadow that had swooped down on her
when she was a young girl picking berries had paid her another visit. What
had all of it meant? Darkness seemed to be attracted to her, or perhaps it
was the other way around? She would have to take a stand at some point,
but which side would she choose? Would she know?

Had Beatrice and Clayton been able to foresee the following days after their
quick exit into the night, they would have realized that they could have
just walked to their next home. Less than a football field away was a parcel
of land that Clayton's estranged mother had purchased a few years prior.

Bored with being a homeowner on a lot that she didn't wish to live on,
keeping it seemed silly and wasteful, so she sold it to her brother, "such
a steal for the price." In turn, he had taken pity on Clayton and his own
wallet and had loftily unloaded the deed to Clayton on an installment plan.

Home sweet home for the next half a century began as a four-hundred-square foot tar-paper ammo shack built by a sniper who sat stubbornly in a swamp surrounded by cattails, thick rows of cornstalks, and plowable land.

All two acres of it were prime real estate, according to Clayton's uncle. "A lot of opportunity right there." The house had two rooms that would serve as a living and cooking area and a bedroom to sleep in. The dilapidated outhouse behind the property served as the place a man could go to have some privacy. There was no running water, and indoor plumbing would have to come much later when money permitted. All in all, it was four weathered walls with a few grimy windows that hadn't seen actual sunlight through them in at least a decade or more. A home, unsettling and macabre at best.

Beatrice's contractions started slowly at first. She had been sweeping out the front room when a gush of water ran down her legs into her dirt pile.

She had hoped that she could get her house in order before her hands would be busy with another responsibility. The growing baby inside of her demanded her attention then and there. She hadn't been able to look upon the pregnancy as a blessing of motherhood but more with an odd sort of disconnect. Maybe she would warm up to being a mother; she would just have to see.

Curtis was born the regular way—head first, under bright lights and screaming from the slap to his backside. "A healthy pair of lungs on that boy," the hospital doctor remarked as he headed out of their room, off to his next delivery. Curtis would soon learn that the only excusable squalling would have to be done during his short hospital stay. As if on cue, he belted out another screech that could be heard resonating down the busy hospital corridors.

The only prerequisite for release from the hospital after the birth of a child was the mother was required to take her newborn with her when she left. In the 1950s, giving birth didn't stretch out into an overnight stay, nor require any of the new gadgets like car seats and carriers in order to leave with the new arrival. Clayton, being a man of sound mind and snap judgment, had seen to bringing a cardboard box to the hospital to carry his son home in. As if bringing home a new kitten or puppy, he loaded his flesh and blood into the box and home they went.

Curtis was a good boy who didn't demand much attention. He followed his parents with his eyes from the safety of his cardboard box, which also served as his makeshift bed. As the months unfolded, Curtis began to reach milestones common to a six-month-old; he started to babble and entertain himself. The box could no longer contain him. Crawling helped to trim away the hours of boredom he faced day after day from being neglected.

He was fed and changed with no other contact, and time crept on. As he started to mouth out sounds and words, he stumbled upon one that got his mother's attention, "Mama." Curtis, small and innocent, had chosen the perfect word that might offer him a hint of protection from her as he grew. Sadly, had Curtis been able to express his deepest needs, had there been one word that would have summed up his existence, his first word would have been "help."

Chapter 22

BRUISES

The greater the power, the more dangerous the abuse.
—Edmund Burke

At first, the warm sweet liquid dripped slowly. Drop by drop, drizzling downward from the top of Beatrice's forehead, moving its stream steadily toward her thighs. Its rich iron content made her senses come alive as she inhaled deeply, absorbing its scent into her lungs. A calmness washed over her as her breathing became slow and organized. Her body was in rhythm with death, enrobed in its lust. As if sensing her need, her uncontrollable yearning, the blood began to flow in a more deliberate stream, acquiescing to her desires. Beatrice opened her mouth slightly. She had to taste its perfection, let it coat the inside of her cheek, caress her tongue, and lastly flow down her throat. Finality was hers to control, a puppet master tugging on eternity's strings.

A noise, off in the distance, pulled her up and away from her cherished world. Her needs faded to the background as she heard the sound intruding into her private space again and again. With senses now engaged with her immediate surroundings, Beatrice sat up and realized that she had fallen asleep and the sounds had been Curtis screaming from outside.

Beatrice had forgotten in her slumber that she hurt from head to toe. She actually thought that her jaw was fractured as some of her upper teeth behind her right cheek felt lose in their sockets. The bruises that were covering her back, breasts, and legs felt hot to the touch from the intense swelling of full-blown purple. Her dress lay torn and violated, dirty from the dragging it received before and after it had cloaked her body. Yes, Beatrice was a mess, and she had Curtis to thank for it.

Beatrice yanked Curtis up by the upper portion of his arm, his feet rising slightly off the ground. He had managed to wander off into the yard and had taken a tumble on the ground, scraping his knee. "All that hollering for a scrape?" Beatrice's tone must have been enough to alert Curtis to his danger, as he went silent. Beatrice had tried to be a fit mother, but all she had received so far was a beating from Clayton for it. Trying to keep Curtis out of sight when Clayton was home was a hell of a lot harder with Curtis crawling and trying to walk. It was all Beatrice could do to keep up with him during the day when Clayton was out earning a living for the family.

Someday it would be Curtis's turn to take the beating for her. Someday she would expect Curtis to be standing in front and not the other way around.

Beatrice had needed a break, away from Curtis and away from Clayton. It was all she could do to gather her thoughts up in the morning and carry them through the day. She had jumped at the chance for a few hours of freedom when her oldest sister offered to let Curtis come and play with his cousin one afternoon. No one need find out that she had a few hours to herself.

Her only misfortune would be having to pick Curtis up again. She had sweet-talked the car from Clayton, telling him that Curtis needed a checkup for his colic at the doctor's office. With keys in hand, Beatrice's feet barely touched the ground as she loaded Curtis in the car and pulled out of the yard.

Clayton hadn't any idea that Beatrice was secretly taking a few hours, off from her duties at home. He would have demanded that Beatrice grab some gloves and help him in the woods instead. The only one privileged to any form of indulgence was Clayton, and he would have been furious had he known that he had not been asked permission. Beatrice was his woman and was not to be seen "running the roads."

LaRosa had been trying to find Beatrice ever since he had stopped by her house and been told by her mother that she had run off and married someone else. He had hoped that wasn't true and wouldn't believe it until Beatrice had told him herself. He had loved her so and felt heartbroken at the unwelcome news. He hadn't expected to see her at the four-way stop on his way into town. LaRosa needed to know the truth, to begin to forget and maybe hold her just one last time.

Beatrice had missed Chocolate Eyes so much. Their passion in the backseat last summer had been so gentle and tender. Unlike Clayton, who couldn't keep an erection unless he was drunk and abusive, Chocolate Eyes had been a find that she had given up, a regrettable loss that she would carry forever. Maybe one last time, for both of them, she thought.

Chocolate was a sinful delight, so decadent to the taste, leaving her craving more when it was all gone, a weakness not to be openly shared but to be savored quietly. Beatrice knew of this indulgence as well as its opponent, its adversary, called sacrifice. Sacrifice had been a constant companion since the words, "I do," drifted from her mouth. Months later, it would be a toss-up as to which of the two the child she was carrying inside of her womb would remind her of. October would bring Curtis a sibling and another responsibility for Beatrice.

Chapter 23

AMEN

"We need to get some Goddamn religion in our house." Clayton's thoughts rattled around in his head. Hoisting feed bags for the local grain and feed store had been Beatrice's idea. Clayton had gotten washed out of the logging business for a few weeks after the rains had set in and the money had gotten too tight to wait for drier weather.

"Never fucking again," Clayton muttered to himself. Rage mixed with adrenaline and innate strength allowed Clayton to handle the eighty-pound grain bags, two at a time. The man that he was required to answer to was a weasel, a yellow canary. Barking orders at Clayton was one of his favorite pastimes. It didn't matter that the job was the same damn thing, day after day; Clayton got a new set of instructions every morning like clockwork.

Clayton had accidentally busted open a bag of hog feed one afternoon, and as it was pouring out onto the floor, Clayton had sworn that he had seen some dried-up, jerky-like pieces of old canary spilling out of the bag mixed in with the corn and grain. He had taken to laughing so hard that Yellow Canary had threatened to fire him then and there. Maybe Clayton would have to come back to that image in the future when he quit.

Some of the old-timers who came into the store had taken a liking to Clayton. They could see that he was a hard worker and a man who kept to himself. Occasionally, one would offer up a chew to Clayton, and he would pack his cheek so tightly with the tobacco that he wasn't quite able to close his lips all the way around it. Somehow it helped to drown out the sound of Yellow Canary's voice, or maybe it just kept the rage inside of him busy for a little while.

Clayton hoisted and thought and hoisted and thought. He had never been inside a church before. His grandmother who raised him had said, "You haven't been invited in by the Lord." Clayton would watch her and his grandfather head out every Sunday morning to go worship God, never asking him to come along. Maybe there had been a list of those Catholics welcomed in and those not. He might have to visit with Mr. Preacher Man one day and find out who else was on the list. Maybe if he got some religion, his luck would turn around? It seemed that his grandparents had come out pretty good, toting their Bible and all. They had done some awful shit to him, and yet they still were on the list. Maybe the bad shit got crossed off every Sunday and Monday started off with a clean slate. He would have to do more figuring, but one thing was for certain, they would get some Goddamn religion starting in their house that evening.

Every Wednesday and Sunday, if you tuned the radio just right, you could hear the Lord's name mentioned over and over. It seemed like religion had found the airways. Maybe too many folks hadn't made the list. Luckily for Clayton, his thoughts had come together on a Wednesday and he was going to get the opportunity to introduce Beatrice and Curtis to Jesus that night. He wasn't sure just how much convincing Beatrice was going to need, but he had thought of several ways to get her attention if he had to.

Clayton was in a good mood as he turned the old four-door into his yard.

Dinner would be cooking for him, and Curtis would have already been fed.

He would see to it that Curtis hadn't been put to bed yet, as that night, they were going to spend some family time together.

Beatrice had sensed something was different about Clayton. Maybe he had polished off a pint of brandy on his way home? He hadn't even bitched when she had failed to crisp the salt pork to his liking or when his fried potatoes had accidentally slid down, touching the green beans on his plate.

When all was quiet in the house, that usually meant a storm was brewing inside of Clayton, usually an ugly, violent storm. Beatrice would have to just wait and see what storm clouds would come.

Clayton, after several attempts, finally found the right station that aired *The Deliverance from Sin*. Outside of a little static and interference, the message the preacher man was saying could be heard throughout the living room. It was time that Beatrice and Curtis learned their place with God.

It took some convincing with a backhander to Beatrice and a kid-size slap across the face for Curtis, but before long, the both of them had warmed up to kneeling in front of the radio for the ninety-minute sermon that they would hear twice a week until the calluses thickened up on their knees and Clayton was assured that he would be saved.

Yes, religion was going to wipe the slate clean for Clayton.

Chapter 24

WHAT BIG BROWN EYES YOU HAVE

Second go-round shot out much like the first one. The only difference was Beatrice knew what to expect when her water broke. Tony was born with a smile on his face, a good-natured little shaver with big brown eyes and a tuft of jet-black hair that stood straight up and out. Tony had his mother's coloring, a nice pigmented, olive-skinned boy, who almost looked a bit jaundiced under the bright lights of the delivery room.

Clayton noticed right off that his light skin and blue eyes were nowhere to be found on his second child. He figured that his "darker" child must have come out looking like Beatrice and that there was nothing he could do about it. It would just make it harder to feel anything for him, knowing his own good looks wouldn't be staring back up at him whenever he looked at Tony.

Times had gotten harder, and now with another mouth to feed, Clayton was starting to feel the strain of responsibility. He had quit the feed store, as too many eyes would have been on him had Canary flown the coop or ended up in a hog trough. Being smart meant being careful. Fortunately, the logging roads had dried up, and he was able to head back to camp with the others. Clayton had been asking around if anyone knew of some land for sale that he might be able to put a down payment on. Still, without a truck, his plans would be limited and his opportunities would be fewer. He had to find a way to buy a truck. "How the hell will that ever happen supporting a family?"

An idea had sneaked up on him one night when he had put Beatrice to work servicing him. With so little to work with, she had kept busy for over an hour, trying to coax him up, giving Clayton a lot of time to think and sort out the details of his plan. If Beatrice had it in her to spend an hour at a time giving blow jobs to Clayton, then surely, she could be servicing other men as well. Clayton had heard that there was good money to be made in sex. He had seen it often enough after payday in the logging camps. Sluts had come out like fireflies once the men's paychecks had been turned into spendable cash. Why shouldn't he get a piece of that action? He would have to find the right way to bring it up. He couldn't risk her getting mad and him ending up having to explain why he had to kill her. What would he do anyway, having to tote two brats around all day?

Clayton's chest pains hit right after the blackberry crow's nest cake had been served up. Clayton had found that Beatrice was handy in the kitchen.

When he had the time, he would teach her some new recipes. He waited until he had taken a couple bites of cake before he clutched his chest and leaned forward. Beatrice jumped out of her chair, scared that Clayton was having a heart attack. Clayton saw his chance and decided to milk it for all it was worth.

Too much work was killing him. He didn't know if he could go on being the only breadwinner in the family. There had to be a way for him to live long enough to see his kids grown. There would only be so many times that he could face those chest pains before the pains would bury him six feet under and Beatrice would be all alone to raise their children. There was something that she could do to keep their family together. It would require her talents and her skills. In the end, she could help keep her husband alive and her family together. Maybe they could even set aside some money to buy a truck so Clayton could haul logs to Canada for himself.

Beatrice hesitated, unsure of what type of trap Clayton was setting for her. She had asked him to repeat himself when he finally had gotten to the part about sex for money. Up until then, she had only been with two men and now her husband wanted to sell her out to strangers?

Clayton assured Beatrice that what she would be doing was going to be okay with God. "After all, the dirty son of a bitches would pay for it from somebody else anyway." Beatrice wouldn't be sinning, as her husband had asked her to do it and Clayton would help her sort out the dirty bastards for God. "Help bring the sinners out in the clearing so God could see them better."

Beatrice cleared the table and checked on the boys now sleeping in their corner of the living room. She had awaken that morning just like every other miserable morning, her life predictable. Now, things were changing, and she needed to make plans. Sex with Clayton hadn't been anything tender or special anyway. She figured that most men would be just like him.

"Sorting for God," that did have a nice ring to it. It seemed like there should be a way to make them repent once they had paid up and the deed was done.

Did God want them to teach them a lesson too?

Chapter 25

ARRANGEMENTS AND DISTRACTIONS

Selling his wife out to strangers was big business for Clayton. He had found that most men wouldn't haggle down the twenty-dollar price tag he had put on Beatrice's head. Clayton demanded payment at the time of service from all of the johns. A few times, he had run across a taker who didn't want to pay up when the time came. Clayton found a way to get even for the aggravation and the lost dollars by fulfilling his other need, a service that he would provide at no additional cost, choking the life out of the cheap son of a bitch.

The need for total control was insatiable, an obsession with Clayton, a fiery beast that never strayed away from its master, always waiting, always watching. Clayton believed that God had given him a pair of powerfully strong hands, and he enjoyed using them in unspeakable ways.

Someday, he would let Beatrice watch what happened to men who didn't make good on their debts. For the time being, he wanted to keep it all to himself. It was a treat he would share when the time came. But for now, he had a truck to buy and nothing was to get in the way of that.

Beatrice's sister had become a little suspicious as to why she was being asked to watch Curtis and Tony so often. The busybody had flatly refused to take the boys any other time besides Saturday afternoons. It really hadn't made any difference in the end anyway, as Beatrice and Clayton had begun leaving the boys unattended for long stretches of time. As long as no one came across a toddler out in the road at midnight, all would be well.

Clayton and Beatrice always made sure that both boys were fast asleep before they would head out for the night.

"The boogeyman only goes looking for boys who aren't asleep and not in their beds."

In between Beatrice's business deals, Clayton managed to fill his spare time shuffling cards with some of the regulars at the Corner Tavern. It wasn't their company that he sought but their tangible goods. It made no difference to him whether the goods were in the form of drinks, paper money, or the occasional property that made its way into the center ring of the poker table.

Conversation was just a required nuisance that he had to accept and bed down with if he was to keep the opportunities coming in his direction.

Clayton knew that most people felt a little uncomfortable around him. It was one way to ensure that he always had the upper hand, the advantage.

People were rarely inclined to share their opinions while in the company of Clayton. Even though he didn't strike up conversation, that didn't mean he had an aversion to hearing himself talk. Once liquored up, Clayton could spin the biggest tales and talk a blue streak. As long as the others kept their mouths shut, listened, seemed interested, and didn't try to interrupt him, well, they would get along just fine.

On one particular night, the cards were running especially hot for Clayton.

He had a knack for reading people and the cards they had in their hands.

Clayton's sixth sense for opportunity always seemed to stretch a lot further than most men's wallets. Along with a sizeable amount of cash already out on the table, some damn old fool had thrown down the keys to his old, rusted-out piece-of-shit pickup truck that had stalled out in the tavern parking lot.

"All in" was just fine with Clayton, especially after he pulled his third ace, king high, and he knew the pot was his.

It was downright amusing to Clayton to see the look of defeat on other people's faces. He always preferred it to laughter. Defeat had a tune all of its own.

In the end, the old clunker had gotten the last laugh. It hadn't taken a half a tank of gas before it left him stranded on the side of the road after a long day in the woods. Had it not been for his stash of twenty-dollar bills that were buried out back in a jar, Clayton might have taken exception to that card game. Fortunately, the time had come for Clayton to put an offer on a flatbed truck capable of hauling logs to Canada. Life was finally starting to travel on solid ground for Clayton.

The brand-new truck looked like a million bucks sitting out in front of his tar-paper shack. The new tires barely had a smudge on them, and the paint was so glossy you could almost make out the color of Clayton's eyes looking through its side panels. Clayton was glad that his wife had a big mouth, as it had finally paid off for him. This new rig was his, and the only other thing missing was a couple men to handle the driving and the lifting.

Clayton needed a crew.

While enjoying a few too many beers later that night, in celebration of his new status, Clayton started up a conversation with two rough lookers by the names Jim and Ray, who had edged their way over to where Clayton was sitting. He had instantly taken a disliking to the lanky son of a bitch who bragged about his brute strength and overall know-how. Clayton had Jim's number the moment words had come out of his mouth, along with a good sense of what a cat must feel like when he traps a mouse under his paw and takes to playing with it for a while before he gets bored and rips its flesh away. Clayton had just found himself a new toy.

Jim was a man who liked the view from his favorite vantage point, on the back of whomever he found he could manipulate. He was a strange man with strange features. His oversized head sat up on the top of a pencil-thin body connected to long, slender legs. He had a few names that had stuck on him like glue, on account of his build. Tootsie Pop and Slim Jim were the most popular. Slim Jim was a smooth talker who could talk a man out of his shirt if it suited his needs. He had taken up residency with his wife and kids, however many of them, and had seen to it to bring in another family to split the costs. It hadn't mattered that between the twelve of them jam-packed in the little rental house that comfort had taken a backseat to the bottom line. What truly mattered to Jim was he didn't have to put all his own money into supporting his brood.

Ray had stumbled into Jim while working at one of the logging camps in between a couple of full-blown drinking binges. Ray was an A+ alcoholic who had spent a great deal of time perfecting his talents. He wasn't a bad man, just a man who had lost his way on account of his view had gotten skewed from looking through the green glass of a Muscatel bottle or from peering over the top lip of a big-mouth Peels beer. Ray never had any intentions of raising his kids in a dirty, filthy, fly-infested house, nor did he want to believe that his wife was getting pregnant regularly to keep upping the monthly welfare check and food stamp limits. He had been hesitant to share a rental house with Jim, but times had been rough and staying sober hadn't been working for him. He knew that if he dried up, he would have to deal with the fact that he had no backbone to stand up on. Ray didn't like to make waves, so staying drunk was a whole lot safer.

Ray and Jim had found work clearing scrub brush out of the way of the camp roads. Ray could work hard if he kept sober, so the trick had always been to keep Ray and the bottle at opposite ends of the woods. Neither man felt that he was being paid a fair wage, and they had both been on the lookout for someone who needed hired help.

After several rounds of brandy and beers, Clayton saw the opportunity to make his move. Before the open sign went out for the night on the front window of the Corner Tavern, Clayton had convinced Ray and Jim to sign on and work for him at half the pay they were making clearing scrub brush.

Clayton was going to like being boss. Yes, he was going to like it very much.

Chapter 26

AUNT AND ANTS

Beatrice had a knack for bringing in the money. It had given her a sense of identity, a feeling of worth; plus she was actually enjoying her work.

Clayton was in charge of hand-selecting the men that she would work on.

He would carefully select them from the bars, making sure to stay away from the coloreds. Sometimes he would stay and watch, and other times, he would be just outside the door whether it be a car door or a motel door. It made no difference to him.

Beatrice had noticed that Clayton seemed different when he stayed around to view the final outcome. She would sense that he didn't want to leave, didn't want to go even after the zipper had been retrieved and yanked up. It made Beatrice a little uneasy that Clayton had the same lustful look during those moments for the john as he did for her on the rare night he was able to get off. But business was business, and Beatrice kept to the script regardless of how handsome the john was or how odd Clayton got after the work was done.

The boys were growing steadily with Curtis nearly two and Tony now a toddler of one, stumbling along on his newly capable legs. Both boys had a sixth sense for staying away from Clayton when the clouds rolled in. Bad weather usually meant beatings for Beatrice, so the boys stayed undercover.

It didn't matter if the weather outside their four walls was beaming with sunshine; the weather indoors could be the storm of all storms. Bad weather was always a threat and never, ever predictable.

The new truck had been the perfect distraction for Clayton. He had spent long hours working in the woods. With income coming both from Beatrice and Canada, he was able to buy up some land that was officially his to strip for lumber. Clayton took to working his land up on the hill, and Beatrice took to working up the land behind the house, tilling it up into a vegetable garden.

From a stranger's point of view, it seemed like life was all brown-eyed Susans and honey for the little family. Had anyone taken the time, they would have unraveled the real truth, which would have had the whole town talking, especially the local sheriff.

The warmer weather was working its magic in the vegetable garden, and Beatrice was pulling tomatoes and cucumbers off the vines in bushel loads.

Her youngest sister had stopped by to check on Beatrice and to admire her gardening skills when their discussion turned to picnics and outings.

Beatrice had never been on a picnic. She had heard a lot about them and wondered how she could convince Clayton to take her on one. Other than bars, Clayton had a shortfall of interests, so picnicking wouldn't be an easy sell.

Clayton had come home early from the woods, feeling good about his accomplishments. He had managed to keep Jim and Ray working hard, and the trips to Cornwall with loads of logs were paying off. He had found a way around the scales at the various checkpoints into the country by learning what the Indians who ran them liked to drink. Just like with any other group of people, you just had to find their weak spot. Clayton could relate quite well to being thirsty, so he always picked up two of each at the liquor store and miraculously, his haul was never too heavy or out of balance.

Clayton wondered what was coming when Beatrice put a generous spread of vegetables and pork on his dinner stand that evening. Good meals usually came with favors and questions so he was prepared for her. When the word *picnic* came out of Beatrice's mouth, Clayton thought he was going to laugh.

How funny it was that his wife would rather eat on the ground than eat in their house without all of the bugs and insects. He had spent all day swatting at deer- and horseflies, and now he was coming home to this nonsense?

Well, if Beatrice wanted a picnic, then by damn, he was going to give her exactly what she asked for. He would see to it that she would always remember their time on the ground, picnicking.

The next day, Beatrice worked hard to get the boys dressed and ready to go meet their dad at the woodlot to have their first picnic together. She had been surprised that Clayton had suggested that they have one right away, as he didn't want her to have to wait a day longer. They would share an early lunch picnic, and then he would go back to work. Beatrice was elated with the notion of acting like other folks as she prepared her best macaroni salad, chicken legs, and crow's-nest cake to take with her. The weather was perfect, she thought, as she grabbed a sheet from the bed, the next best thing to a tablecloth.

After some family time and full bellies, today might be the day to share the rest of her news with Clayton, Beatrice figured as she finished packing up the car. She knew she would be showing soon, and Clayton didn't like surprises. Yes, Beatrice had a strong feeling that today would be one day she wouldn't soon forget.

Clayton had already picked out a spot when Beatrice pulled the old four-door into the clearing. He had a grin from ear to ear, which Beatrice mistakenly took for a good mood. He was quick to take the sheet from under her arms as he ushered the boys over to where they were going to enjoy their picnic. While Clayton spread out the makeshift picnic blanket, Beatrice smiled and proceeded to lay out their noontime meal on top of it.

"Make yourselves all cozy and comfortable." Clayton smiled down on his family, choosing not to sit down and join them. "I want you to have a real picnic, firsthand."

As if on cue, from the smell of the food and the stirring up of their mound, millions of red ants swarmed over top of the sheet onto Beatrice's feet, legs, torso, and arms. The boys started to swat and scream as they too were bitten by Clayton's picnic companions. Clayton's plan had worked perfectly. It had been hard finding the perfect spot, the biggest mound, but he had done it. Clayton couldn't stop laughing at his brilliant stunt.

Beatrice jumped to her feet, dragging the boys with her. She didn't know if she was more afraid of Clayton or more furious at him. The ants were still biting and getting caught in the folds of her clothes.

"Damn you to hell, Clayton!" she spat out with venom. She would pay for her lack of respect, but for now she didn't care. "Just a frigging picnic is all I asked of you."

As she ran toward the car, Beatrice yelled back, in the direction of where Clayton stood watching, "By the way, I am pregnant again, and why don't you wipe that shitty-ass grin from your face?"

That was the last picnic outing Clayton's family ever had.

Chapter 27

BETRAYAL

I know a bank where the wild thyme blows,
Where oxlips and the nodding violet grows
Quite overcanopied with luscious woodbine,
With sweet musk-roses and with elgantine.
—Shakespeare

Beatrice managed to gather her wits over the picnic incident and allowed it to go unchallenged once she gave it some intelligent thought. Her life had been a fight, a war that began back in the cradle that sat on her mother's front porch. A smart girl like her needed to sharpen her sword and become smarter than Clayton, think more like him and then beyond, beyond reproach. Her cleverness was what had gotten her through rough times before. This challenge would be no different. She was designed to be sneaky, to hold back emotion, to take, and even to win in the end. Yes, she was indeed crazy like a fox, and she would live up to her namesake.

The first night Beatrice split open the foil wrapper encasing the over-the-counter sleeping pills, her hands began to shake. It was a toss-up as to whether her trembling was from fear or just innate excitement. She knew Clayton was going to sleep deeply and soundly and all with her help. No matter that his tank had been filled with nearly a quart of brandy, she would help to soothe his rage by drugging him with sleep aids.

If she crushed the pills into a fine powder, they would dissolve nicely into a glass of milk or in a pinch, even in a glass of tomato juice. The latter occasionally bubbled up and risked overflowing Beatrice's secret. Too much acid in the juice made it questionable.

Clayton, from day one of his new "after-hours cocktail," never caught on to Beatrice's cleverness. Up through the years and even to his death, his sleeping pills would rock him to sleep most nights with Clayton none the wiser. Beatrice had found a friend at the five-and-dime.

The night her contractions sprang a leak, Clayton had been sleeping for nearly a full hour. Beatrice had become accustomed to the stages of childbirth and almost felt bored with its progress. Had the pain of childbirth not been so riveting and unpredictable as she continued to dilate, she might have just stayed at home and let the babies simply pop out whenever they were destined to do so. No fanfare would be required, no change in routine. Frankly, Beatrice would have much rather settled for birth control if Clayton would have allowed her.

Alice was born on a beautiful, clear fall afternoon. Her blue eyes were large and alert and shone like aquamarine gems in the white light of the hospital overheads. Wisps of angel hair swept over her tiny little head, and her dainty fingers looked like they belonged on a china doll.

It hadn't really occurred to Beatrice that baby number 3 might be a girl. Medicine in that era didn't lend itself to knowing the sex of a fetus inside a mother's womb. Beatrice began to feel uncomfortable about her changing family. Boys had been predictable, and eventually she would make them earn their keep by protecting her when the time came. A girl didn't feel right to her. A stir of jealousy cleared her mind from the exhaustion of pushing. Little girls were temptations and home wreckers. She knew that Clayton would be unable to resist.

Clayton's mood had lifted after the grogginess faded from his interrupted slumber. The hospital nurse rushed out to the lobby where he sat slumped against a wall, jubilantly announcing the birth of his daughter. As the meaning of the words began to sink in, Clayton realized with a stir of excitement that he had a brand-new, untouched little girl of his very own.

He would train her well, and she would always be his. Beatrice could tend to the family business, and he could tend to his new little wonder. Alice was going to be his property, bought and paid for. One day, they would walk side by side, arm in arm. Beatrice would then find her place, which would be a couple of steps behind the both of them. Yes, he was going to enjoy raising a girl, one who could bring in top dollar when the time came. Yes, this one would be his forever, to have and to hold.

Chapter 28

CRAWL SPACE

With three young children all under the age of four, life in the tiny two-room shack was close to unbearable. Clayton had threatened, during many of his evening tirades, that if they weren't careful, he might just burn down the goddamn thing with Beatrice and the boys in it. He wasn't ready to part with Alice in the flames though, at least not yet; he still had high hopes for her, plans for the future, the moment he felt that Beatrice had overstayed her welcome.

In spite of the fact that Beatrice's body was beginning to show the effects of motherhood and her tight waist was fighting gravity from pushing three babies out in such a short time, the johns still loved her. Even when she was clearly showing, there were men who were so turned on by her womanhood that they wanted her again and again. *Twenty dollars, please.* Luckily for Beatrice, that business was still lucrative, as it made her a little more valuable to keep around.

A good mood had cornered Clayton one spring morning, giving him an idea to add on to his living space. A couple of bedrooms and maybe a kitchen might help to spread his miserable bunch out, giving them a few hundred feet more to move around in. With a little money put aside from Beatrice's handiwork, Clayton got the notion of putting Ray and Jim to work digging out a proper cellar, one they could stand up in and get some good use out of. There wouldn't be any need for fancy stuff, just some cement blocks, floorboards, sturdy frames, and a little drywall. They wouldn't have time to be too particular or concerned about water tables or proper leveling, as the spring rains were threatening weeklong downpours.

Building a basement in the center of low-lying land that took on the looks of a boggy creek in the springtime wasn't the most intelligent thing Clayton had thought of. But, by damn, once he made a decision about something, there wasn't any reasoning left to be done. Clayton was going to have it, and have it he did. He would later find that for the next fifty years or so, he would have to sump pump the hundreds of gallons of water that filled his basement like a fish tank every spring, but that would only be after he stocked it with bullhead and fished through the early summer months.

"A man has to make his own kind of entertainment."

The crawl space, shaped like a crescent moon, lay directly underneath the original part of the house. From the indentations of its inner walls, it almost looked like it had been dug out with a kitchen spoon or at best a small ash shovel. The height of the entrance to the crawl space was a little over three feet with the depth reaching out to the far end of the house. All in all, the peculiar, odd-shaped, tomb-like space extended itself about ten feet from one end to the other, including its curved middle. At some point, there must have been an entrance leading into its belly from the outside, a spot long covered up with dirt and soil. Oddly, the dirt that made up the crawl space was completely different from the dirt unearthed while digging out the full cellar.

Unlike the freshly tilled soil, the crawl space was comprised of a deeply rich, rusty-brown-colored earth.

Clayton felt sure that this little find would come in handy at some point.

He liked hiding places and hiding things, and this would be as good a spot as any. He was quite pleased with his new discovery and considered this private space in the cellar off limits to everyone but himself.

Projects done well took care and patience, neither being traits that had ever been used to describe Clayton, not even on a good day. With little time spent on the finer details of home renovations, Clayton was able to put together about five hundred extra square feet of livable space in no time at all. Somehow between the alcohol binges and the temper tantrums, the drywall had actually survived, mostly unscathed. It was a day worth celebrating when Clayton had driven the last nail into a door casing.

The emotional storm that bore down on Beatrice, Curtis, Tony, and Alice during the home improvements was clearing again. Even when all was quiet, a short break usually meant the storm was simply resting in order to pick up and build more momentum.

Chapter 29

STILLBORN

With thousands of acres of uncleared forest for the taking, land was selling for cheap. As if playing a strategic game of Monopoly, Clayton set out purchasing properties two at a time. Ownership was power, and power was always all-consuming to Clayton.

Ray continued to earn his keep, working hard for Clayton. He had a knack for putting everything he had into staying busy. Learning early on that his new employer had a temper, he felt safer keeping a good distance away. His pay had skimped down to next to nothing, even with the increased workload. Clayton had begun substituting "cold ones with twist tops" in place of paper money and had also started to offer up Beatrice for the standard fee, all to recoup any exchange of actual wages paid. It was a good thing that the roar of the chainsaw helped to block out some of the disturbing turn of events that Ray was caught up in. Noise to drown it all out in the daylight and twist-offs to drown out the rest of the demons.

Jim managed to keep up with his own workload when he wasn't busy running his mouth. With an affinity for the spoken word, he could have carried on all day if Clayton would have let him. Jim survived a few close calls before he realized the potential of Clayton's wrath. A couple of times, Clayton's chainsaw had come dangerously close, close enough to snag the denim on Jim's pant legs. Jim knew that accidents could happen out in the woods, and his survival instincts told him that probably more so around Clayton.

With never a shortage of work needing to be done, Clayton had demanded Beatrice's time be split equally between a garden hoe and a wood hook during the dry weather of the summer months. Working in the woods and tending to three small children was no easy task for Beatrice. The boys were old enough now to fetch water jugs, move equipment, and haul some of the smaller trees that had to be cleared away. Not yet in kindergarten, there was a good part of the day when the boys could make themselves useful. Alice was still too young to carry her own weight and spent her time either under the blue sky tethered to a tree so she couldn't wander off or confined to the backseat of the truck. Beatrice had come close to leaving her a couple of times, but at the last moment, she had thought better of it. She hated the competition but knew Clayton would kill her if he had found his prize possession absent from the back of the truck when he got home.

With no shortage of wildlife, it wasn't uncommon to come across a bear or two, especially early spring after a winter hibernation. New with cubs, female bear ventured out, hungry and curious. With the secretive test by the government of crossbreeding coyotes and wolves, a mixed variety of both traveled in packs, running through the dense forest. Yes, home among the woodland creatures was always an amazing experience, as long as you didn't wander off too far away from the protection of the human pack.

The hard work helped to bulk up the muscles of Beatrice's biceps. It felt good to her to sweat out the fear and fury that always had her nerves on overdrive. Physical work tamed the need to pull out her hair strand by strand, which was exactly what she did when her body was left to idle for too long. She had been too busy to pay attention to the nagging upset stomach that had found her with a vengeance one hot August afternoon.

Pregnant again, Beatrice had been relieved when the morning sickness had passed a few months prior. With all the lifting she had done, she assumed that maybe she had pulled her back out and the uncomfortable feeling was just making its way around to the rest of her.

It wasn't until the blood, warm and sticky, began to drizzle down her legs that she understand the magnitude of her situation, Beatrice was giving birth in the middle of the woods. With no time to alert Clayton or make her way to the hospital, Beatrice squatted right where she stood and pushed out a small infant. The newborn lay lifeless on the ground among a bed of leaves and dirt. Beatrice realized that the child was a stillborn. Withholding a name, a prayer, or a cloth to shelter the tiny child, Beatrice shrugged her shoulders, uprighted herself, and left the dead infant on the ground to be retrieved later by the wood's wildlife. Beatrice could already feel her spirits lifting.

Chapter 30

CROWN CURTIS KING

Curtis began kindergarten with a mixed sense of relief. Time away from the house would be a new experience for him. He had been forewarned numerous times by his mother to keep his mouth shut. If the people at school found out about all the badness he created at home, they would put him in jail. Already a bundle of confusion and fear, Curtis knew his only salvation would be to stay quiet. In the mind of a five-year-old, it all came down to you talk, you die.

Beatrice was all too happy to send Curtis out the door for a couple of hours each day. Having one less child underfoot might help with the knots that had her all tied up in her head. Clayton's mother had started dropping by on a more regular basis since Curtis was born. For some reason, she had decided that it was her duty to keep up with her grandchild. Curiously, it wasn't all of them she was interested in. In fact, for a while, it was unclear whether or not she actually knew Tony's and Alice's names.

Nanny, an honorary name given by Beatrice to Clayton's mother, wasn't in reference to her caregiving qualities. It came out one afternoon while Beatrice, already in a foul mood, was staring out the back porch, watching the damn goat, loose again and chewing away at her strawberry plants.

Clayton had brought home the creature on account of he wanted the kids to have goat's milk, as it was cheaper than cow's milk. He had sensed that

Beatrice wasn't all too happy with the idea, but it would be just one more frigging way he could get under her skin. Beatrice truly hated that animal.

Two could play that game, she decided; hence Nanny became the children's name for Clayton's mother.

Nanny made quite the show whenever she came across town to see her grandson Curtis. She always brought him at least one present, which he was to open slowly in front of his brother and sister. Usually it was an expensive toy or fancy clothes bought from the specialty shops. On one such occasion, she had a grand piano delivered to the now expanded shack, which took up nearly half of the living area. "Curtis deserves nice things."

After a while, Tony and Alice stopped looking around, hoping that she had brought them a gift too. The only time there was actually something for Tony or Alice was when it was their birthday. Tossed in the backseat of Nanny's car would be an unwrapped flannel shirt for Tony or a hideous blouse for Alice, neither of which Nanny felt the need to actually carry into the house. No cake, no fanfare, no pretty paper. Whatever the reason, Curtis was the apple of her eye and the rest of the children were the worms.

Beatrice began to wonder if Nanny could be right about Curtis. Maybe he would go on to make his mark in the world. Maybe he would return and pay her back for all of the hardships he created for her. It was too soon to tell, but it was worth it to try to show some favoritism and hope that he was old enough to pick up on it.

Favoritism was the word furthest from Beatrice's mind when she thought of Alice. She didn't dare be too harsh to Alice in front of Clayton because that had already caused her a few beatings. There was nothing stopping her, however, from getting even with her while the two were home together alone. Sending Tony outside to play with the goat, Beatrice would call Alice over to her in a sweet, nonthreatening voice. A small child of three, Alice would run over to her mother only to have the clothes ripped off her back. Standing naked and trembling, Alice would be made to crawl up the ladder that Beatrice kept on the back porch for special occasions and into the attic that lay flush with the ceiling over the living room.

The attic was home to spiders and whatever wasps set up refuge up there. The floor of the attic was never finished so the rafters were the only safety that stood between Alice and the seven-foot drop through the plasterboard to the living room below. Perched on the beams like an injured sparrow, Alice would remain in the attic for hours on end. Tony had interrupted the ritual one day and had become worried that his little sister was up there in the dark all by herself. Beatrice had quickly explained away that Alice needed to learn her ABCs and this way she could concentrate. It wasn't that Beatrice cared whether or not Tony saw but what he might have let slip to Clayton about it later.

Being powerful felt good to Beatrice. It didn't matter to her that her misguided fury had been unleashed on an innocent, helpless child. At least she hadn't killed her. She was the wife, and, by damn, she would never give up her wedding band to anyone. Once the beast inside of her had been exorcised, Beatrice would calmly sit down at her sewing machine. With a cup of her favorite hot tea close at hand, Beatrice, being the good mother, would stitch up another dress for her little girl. Occasionally looking up at the ceiling, Beatrice wondered if Alice really could understand how much her mother truly despised her.

Chapter 31

THE BIRTH OF PATIENCE

Into the land of tiny red teddy bears is where my heart taketh me.
Where truth glistens like diamonds in the sweet syrup streams
and love flows unconditionally amidst my slumbering dreams.
—A. Tacked

Beatrice grew weary as her fourth live birth took its course in the small hospital room. Medications had improved over the years, and she was relieved that the pain came in oozy waves rather than agonizing outbursts like the other toils of labor had been.

"One more mouth to feed, one more load of wash to do."

Beatrice was grateful that God had shown pity on her, giving her almost two pregnant-free years between Alice and the one trying to introduce itself now through the cloudiness of the Percocet. Raising children was a burden, one that Beatrice resented the hell out of. Child-rearing was her responsibility and no one else's. Her own mother had long ago lost track of how many mouths she had fed in between the sleepless nights and the endless and thankless days waiting for Beatrice's siblings to grow up.

"Never" would have been a better idea if the idea had been her own.

Beatrice's primary duties, according to Clayton, came in two forms, prostitution and procreation. Clayton never hesitated to rub her nose in that dirty little fact. The painful truth rippled throughout her body, keeping time with her contractions. Reality was a well-known enemy to Beatrice, and right there on the sterile hospital bed, it was sinking its fangs deep into what was left of her fragile psyche.

The doctor's words would be another death sentence, another power struggle. How excited could she be really? If the doctor said it was a girl, she would be just one more plaything for Clayton. Beatrice hadn't been able to tame her temper, hadn't been able to heal the bitterness that drained out of her like an abscess. She already knew, her intuition never lied, never steered her off course. Beatrice would be sewing a lot more dresses on her old Singer soon enough.

Sadie took her time, progressing with intention, forward moving, rock-steady. Gifted with an uncanny resilience, one day, she would balance the scales between a cage and a home for Beatrice, all on account of patience, guided by the gentle, compassionate hand of Sadie. Another push and a deep breath would make Beatrice a new mother. It was too late to change her predicament now.

A summer baby meant there was still a lot of daylight not to be wasted.

Plenty of time left in the day to fulfill any duties that may have been neglected during her twenty-four-hour absence. Rest wouldn't come easy, so with hoe in hand and a good swallow of painkillers, Beatrice set about working in the garden and tending to everyone else until nightfall took away the last light of her long day.

Meals served were the deciding factor as to how long the well-wishers stayed, pretending to drop by to welcome the new baby. Relatives considered themselves company and usually arrived empty-handed with not so much as a pie or a tuna casserole. Beatrice's own mother had not been up for all the excitement and felt it best to stay away for as long as she possibly could. Empty-nest syndrome had turned into an all-inclusive vacation, and she wasn't ready to part with her free time just yet. Clayton's mother had offered to run by and pick up Curtis. Too much chaos wasn't good for him; it was the same speech she had shared twice before. Curtis didn't deserve to have his home disrupted once again with another kid. Fortunately for everyone, she in particular hadn't offered to bring over a covered dish. Nothing Nanny attempted to cook would be edible anyway. Starving would be a much safer choice.

As the weeks merged into months, Sadie was left in the care of her older sister, Alice. Given the fact that there were less than a handful of years between the two, it wasn't saying much for the responsibility of child care. A woman who lived down the road a slight way put the fear into Beatrice one afternoon that she could go to jail if the state came by and found the children home alone. It wouldn't matter that Beatrice was working hard with her husband to put food on the table, no siree, the law would put her in cuffs and parade her down the road for anyone and everyone to see. As luck would have it for Beatrice, the woman offered up a solution to the problem. Being a Good Samaritan and neighbor, she would come over in the mornings and watch the children for a nominal fee.

Charlotte was a crafty, sneaky, hateful woman who took pleasure in administering punishment for the sake of punishment. She had likely gotten bored torturing small, defenseless animals and had set out looking for a new set of targets to share her kind of affection with. Yes, it would be her job to make the children in the dismal shack camouflaged by swamp cattails the next project of her enjoyment.

Fortunately, Beatrice caught on to Charlotte's actions after a couple of weeks. Wanting to keep misery and torture strictly in the family, Beatrice didn't appreciate anyone else abusing her children. She didn't need the children too stirred up unless she was doing the stirring. The day she came home to see Sadie, still a toddler, kneeling in the corner on top of a splattering of wooden clothespins, she marched Charlotte directly out the door. "I don't need trash like you in my house."

Later in the day, after her former babysitter was shown the door, Beatrice decided that it was time to let Sadie out of the corner. She had to admit the clothespins were a nice touch and she would have to keep them in mind for use at a later date.

With a pair of each, Beatrice set out moving each child like a pawn in the internal chess game she played with Clayton. Just like chess, she knew that the pawns were the most expendable, the sacrifice pieces, because there were more of them. When the woodpile got low or there was work to be done in the woods, Curtis and Tony were moved forward a space. When it was comforting Clayton or keeping house, Alice and Sadie were moved two spaces. Beatrice figured early on in the game that the king was beyond value and losing him meant losing the game. Beatrice may have sacrificed a lot keeping time with the king, but she was never one to give up the game. After all, being queen, she knew she was the most powerful piece on the board anyway.

Chapter 32

FINAL JEOPARDY

A couple of wrenches, a screwdriver or two, smokes, and even a lunch pail had mysteriously disappeared from Clayton's truck. He had been watching things disappear a little at a time for well over a year now. At first, he had blamed Beatrice for moving his things and had even given her a beating or two as a reminder to leave his things the hell alone. She swore to him that she hadn't touched anything and that he probably had a thief on his hands. Clayton had even set some traps for Curtis and Tony to make sure that they were not hiding his things. They had passed the tests, though it annoyed Clayton to no end that he couldn't pin it on either of them.

With Jim and Ray on his payroll off and on for nearly ten years, Clayton started to wonder if it might be one of them. Ray had moved his family out from under Jim and was renting a tiny house from Clayton's mother. Jim hadn't liked it very much that the rent was now his full responsibility, and rumor had it that he was going to be evicted soon enough. Clayton hoped that it wasn't Ray who was stealing from him. Ray was by far the hardest worker of the two and didn't require a lot of explanation if his pay got all fouled up or lost altogether. He decided to put the squeeze on Ray first, as he knew he wouldn't be able to take the pressure of being cornered. One way or the other, Ray would talk.

Sneaking between two elms, Clayton cold-cocked Ray with a punch to the face. After a few minutes, Ray staggered to his feet, wiping the blood from his chin. Clayton wanted answers, and if he had to beat them out of Ray, then lucky him. Ray had been waiting, half expecting a confrontation with Clayton as he had just recently startled Jim, who was rifling through the floorboards of Clayton's truck. Ray had looped back around, remembering that he needed to retrieve his water jug when he caught sight of a guilty Jim.

Ray had pretended not to notice, but by the look on Jim's face, he knew that he had been caught red-handed. Ray didn't want any trouble so he gave Clayton the full story, for better or worse.

The drive back to the house was a harrowing one. Clayton hit the gas pedal with such force that the engine nearly came out from under the hood.

Speed, potholes, fury, and dirt roads do not make good traveling companions.

"That fucking Jim. He's got light fingers, the son of a bitch." Clayton was furious. He began clenching and unclenching his fists, grinding his teeth together in between mouthfuls of brandy. "I'll teach the motherfucker a lesson he will never forget." Clayton spat out the words with such venom that Beatrice became increasingly frightened.

"Get my fucking shotgun from the bedroom," Clayton barked at Beatrice.

With a roll of electrical tape and a spool of baling wire already sitting out on the metal kitchen table, Clayton snatched the gun from Beatrice and set about making sure the barrel was fully loaded. The anger, coupled with his fast, jerky movements, caused his freshly poured shot glass of white lightning to spill over onto the table.

"Come get my shit. I will blow your fucking head right off from your shoulders." Clayton pounded his fist on the table shortly before he swung his elbow out, sending the remaining items on the table sailing into the air.

The children watched from the safety of the fence line that ran alongside the back wall of the chicken coop. Their father was scary enough without a gun. Fear made their knees buckle as they huddled together, silently praying their father wouldn't come looking for one of them to set an example.

Clayton, with gun in hand, stormed toward the truck. First he cracked opened the window about three inches and set about taping and wiring the barrel of the gun to the front seat of the truck. Next he rigged the lever to pull back when the force of the door put tension on the wires he jerry-rigged around the door lever and gun. Clayton would be ready for Slim Jim, and he wouldn't even mind the mess Jim's brain would make when it exploded all over his truck.

"Payback is always a pleasure."

The next morning came with no blood, no body, and no gratification for Clayton. He had eagerly peered out the window off and on all evening, hoping for a little action, but had fallen asleep shortly before morning. If it had not been for Ray warning the children when he saw them sneaking around the truck, wondering what their dad had hidden inside, the Clayton family would have been minus a few. Collateral damage was always a risk but nothing a trip to the woods couldn't have solved. Animals were always good at cleaning up evidence.

Clayton wasn't done with Jim yet. His first plan hadn't worked, but there were other ways to make Jim suffer. Clayton enjoyed taking matters into his own hands, so plan B was taking shape when Jim pulled into the yard, ready to ride with Clayton to the woodlot like each and every other workday.

Jim was a little nervous when Clayton asked him to drive. Seemed the damn clutch was going out on the truck and they wouldn't be loading any wood for a couple of days. "We'll just go out for a couple of hours and mark some trees that will be next in line for Canada," Clayton said, throwing his hands up with his words for added effect.

Jim was having a difficult time keeping his focus and his eyes on the road ahead. It just didn't make sense that Clayton wanted him to drive. Clayton hated riding with anyone, hated anyone having that much control over him.

Something wasn't adding up. Where was Ray? Had he squealed to save his own skin? Jim knew Clayton didn't accept apologies, period. Something was terribly wrong. Warning bells were going off in Jim's head as he struggled with his flight-or-fight senses. He couldn't let Clayton take charge, couldn't allow the woods to be the last thing he would ever see. Adrenalin began to take over rational thought.

The tree that stopped Jim's Chrysler was about one hundred yards off the embankment. Clayton was knocked out cold. Jim, however, had only taken on a broken nose and some cuts from the shards of shattered windshield glass. Jim made it out to the main road where he was able to flag down some help. Jim would see to it that he ended up a hero, or at least he would spin it that way. Everyone would remember the man who tried to save poor Clayton, who unfortunately wouldn't make it out alive.

The hospital thoroughly checked Clayton out. He was lucid and awake and other than an awful headache had only required a few stitches.

Miraculously, he hadn't suffered any internal injuries, but the hospital had found a curious indentation on the back of his skull when they had flipped him over. It seemed that the indentation was the exact size and shape of the head of a large hammer. With the force that it appeared to have hit Clayton, it was surprising that his skull hadn't cracked open like a walnut.

It took a while, but Clayton finally caught up with Jim. Whatever happened that day, Clayton considered the score settled. Even with the bad headaches that would show up periodically for the rest of his life, he said they were even. Jim was never seen or heard from again.

Chapter 33

BABY OF THE FAMILY

I am nobody. Who are you?
—Emily Dickinson

Wising up to the mystifications of ovulation and cycles, Beatrice was able to put six years between Sadie and the next baby in line, me, Helen. April showers bring May flowers right along with another baby girl. I can't really say much about that day in the hospital other than it started with chaos, ended with chaos, and much as it began, continued on for years with the same vigor and intensity for as long as I can remember.

I was born under bright lights at the hand of a doctor who clearly should have let someone else take call that night. Surprisingly, not stopped for driving while intoxicated on his way to the hospital, Mr. Doctor found himself now cornered, pinned against the wall by an angry and also drunk, Clayton. Neither man could have walked a straight line for a pot of gold at the other end of the long hospital corridor, but it burned Clayton to no end that the "fucking doctor was drunk."

Maybe Clayton was never reported for assault because the doctor knew that the beer cologne that reeked from each of his own pores coupled with a drunken swagger might tip off his superiors to an even bigger problem.

Fortunately, he never lost sight of which end was up and regardless of Clayton walking and swearing and walking and swearing directly outside the sterile hospital room, I was delivered for better or worse.

Relieved that his time at the hospital was over, at least until morning, Clayton jumped into his pickup truck and made his way home. The middle of the night was always a good time to wake his brood. He relished seeing their sleep-encrusted eyes and their bewilderment that came with it. No punishment that night, though. Just a "Hip, hip hooray!" for their brand-new little sister, now sleeping soundly in the hospital. The next day, he would bring his third little girl home to meet the family. Life was full of variety for Clayton, and as his family grew, so did his authority over it.

Beatrice had hit the jackpot coming across an old, tired-looking wooden crib at a rummage sale a few months before my arrival. With the other children, she had discovered that cardboard boxes had been self-limiting. A wooden crib with high slats would ensure that I wouldn't be coming out on my own anytime soon.

Staring out at the separate world through the slats of my wooden haven, I felt safe, yet alone, much too young to really make sense of anything. Just a few feet away, the world played before me like a television set tuned in to some kind of horror movie, replaying itself on a continuous loop. The monsters fed me, occasionally talked to me, but monsters will always be monsters, and more than anything, I watched as they chased each other from room to room in front of my crib, screaming, crying, bleeding, and often naked. The loud noises made the world on their side a place of uncertainty and fear. I was glad to be contained, glad for the distance that would remain for the first three or four years of my life.

"Close to a playground worth of children and yet not one of them worth a damn." Motherhood bore down on Beatrice, picking away at her sanity like a scab not ready to be released from its wound. With only one way to fight, one way to survive, Beatrice made a decision; she would plug the hole. Be damned or be dead, she was getting the latest in birth control, an IUD.

If Clayton wanted more children, he would have to do it himself.

Part 3

BETWEEN TWO WORLDS

All that's necessary for the forces of evil to win in the
world is for enough good men to do nothing.
—Edmund Burke

Chapter 34

RULES AND REQUIREMENTS

Thick with rules, home life should have come with its own manual, a disturbing book, filled with pages and pages of rules and demands separated into multiple, horrendous chapters. If ever a book would have been crafted by Clayton, it would no doubt have been written in blood on thin slices of human skin made supple by endless curing and care. The binding would have creaked and moaned each and every time the book was handled, and Clayton would have stroked its cover continuously until its shine became dull. His precious rules so alive, so powerful.

Fear, a primary ingredient in every rule ever written, was always joined by its companions, pain and suffering. The delivery of punishment whenever rules were not strictly followed came swift, unyielding, and irrevocable.

Like a jackal watching and waiting enthusiastically for dinner, Clayton crouched, waited, and delivered his beatings with force and zest. Driving home the reminder our lives were fragile and owned solely by him.

"No niggers, no blondes, no redheads, no Polacks, Paddies, Jews, nor the Canucks that lived just on the other side of the border." Clayton hated them all.

When his list didn't seem extensive enough, he was quick to include prejudices that spread out regionally as well. Adding to his mix of craziness became "no one to the north of our house and no one to the east of our house." Try explaining that to a now four-year-old.

Clayton loathed outsiders. "Just goddamn disposables, throwaways and yellow canaries. Fuck them all straight to hell," he would say when he felt the saying needed to be done.

Clayton was the lord and ruler of his kingdom. All houseguests had to be cleared only through him, no exceptions. This included but was not limited to Jehovah's Witnesses, tax assessors and collectors, drifters, and, by all means, relatives. Any free exchange of conversation between "them" and us had to be first approved, wielded by the gilded gavel of Clayton. Treason was a serious offense and a title given to all unapproved verbal exchanges.

"Keep your fucking mouth shut, or I will shut it for you for good."

Outside of the primary rules, all other rules came in two colors, pink and blue. The brothers were required to wear hats, especially if they were working in the woods. Hair had to be short, military cut, and never, ever below the top of their ears. Shaving was to be done the moment the boys even suspected their first whiskers and every day thereafter. Clean-shaven was the law. In Clayton's regime, he was the only one allowed to go unshaven for an undetermined period of time. Curtis and Tony worked hard in the woods and took their backhanders whenever Clayton felt they were "disrespecting him."

With testosterone came privileges and rewards. Curtis and Tony had freedoms that helped them to blend in with the rest of the world. Both boys were allowed to stay after school and pursue activities and interests. Their work stayed in the woodlot and didn't extend to busy "women's work" at home. As their manhood became more apparent, they would be allowed to date and go out with friends with a reasonable curfew on the weekends.

Clayton had plans for his boys, high hopes—hope partnered with potential and possibilities. Maybe the boys would continue on with the family business and grow like he had, with a thirst for sorting out the bastards of the world into neat little piles. Yes, being male had its advantages and would ensure his namesake, a new ruler to the throne when Clayton was gone.

Pink rules were the most ruthless rules of them all. No frills attached, they came with harshness and hatred and usually a leather belt—working tirelessly in the massive gardens during the growing season and cutting cords of wood in the cooler months, tending to chickens, pigs, beehives, yard work, and housework and to the intimate needs of Clayton. No matter the size of our hands or the single digits of our ages, we worked all the time.

School was our vacation and probably kept us from cracking like Humpty Dumpty.

Being female, our bodies were considered dirty and vile, designed solely as a physical distraction for men or as a replacement for horse and plow in the fields. Cutting our hair was strictly forbidden and makeup was for sluts.

Wearing of a single earring in each lobe was a sign of femininity and was administered and delivered to each sister by way of a bar of soap and needle fumbled in the hands of Clayton while we lay on the old metal kitchen table.

Being branded and marked before we could walk was customary.

Hiding the bruises became a game of wit, a necessity for "noncompliant" children. Backhanders became as common as skinned knees, and threats flowed like brandy in tall water glasses. We learned early on to come when called, and time was measured in seconds and not minutes. Distractions of any sort were simply not tolerated. Pets, people, or personal things could be taken away and destroyed if Clayton believed that our full attention and adoration wasn't focused on him. Clutter had no place in our thoughts, and our minds had to be continuously tuned in to Clayton's needs.

As if violating our bodies wasn't good enough, my sisters and I were rarely called by our given names. Clayton found one more way to strip us of our identities by calling each of us by a nickname that had been thought up after one of his frequent all-night drinking binges. It was important to him that we not be called anything that drew attention to the fact that we were girls. Alice became known as "Speedy Gonzales," after the male mouse from the Warner Brothers' cartoon series. Sadie was named "Togo," after a male wrestler that Clayton had seen on our black-and-white television, and I became "Sam," named after a dog that was the "dumbest fucking dog ever lived." Occasionally, Alice was treated to another name given to her by Beatrice. "Dynamite" was never a name that rolled off Beatrice's tongue when she was in a good mood. Like everything else, names were just another way to pick away at our emotional scabs.

When Clayton wasn't reflecting and stewing in his deep-set hatred for females, he would spend time in an equally dark and dangerous place in his head. Clayton was plagued with paranoia of government intervention. He knew that there were spies at every corner. Being irrational and volatile, he refused to "roll over and play dead" to the government mind-control games.

Never once succumbing to daylight savings time, "Clayton time" lagged behind an hour or sped up an hour, depending on the season. Most times, a few extra minutes would be added, in addition to the full hour just to fool and trick anyone who may have been watching the time, calculating the demise of Clayton's secrets.

"Keep the fuckers guessing."

Rules and requirements kept us his and kept us quiet. Worker bees, busy and alert. No one ever challenged Clayton's rules. There would be no winning against a diabolical man like Clayton. The goal was a simple one. Keep quiet, stay alive, and one day, if we were lucky, we would be free.

Chapter 35

THE WHEELBARROW DRUNK

Your country Cadillac has one wheel
Your seat it does recline
No matter for the dirt no matter for its grime
Forget about the bloodstains, they are not your type
You won't remember by morning
They say it's not your time
Pour you in and pour you out
Bounce between the rows of corn avoiding some of the rocks
At last your country home awaits you, in darkness I dump you out
Never waking, never moving, it's what life is all about.
—A. Tacked

Ray had stumbled upon a rough patch of bad luck. His wife had just kicked him out of the house. Once she realized that she could sign the back of the welfare checks herself, her dependency on Ray diminished. With yet another dollar sign in diapers, money was coming in regularly for the missus. In her eyes, Ray was quickly becoming just a nuisance to have around. Sleeping on the floor in the front room of their tiny rental house had quickly turned into "call before you come over."

The two of them hadn't really known what to do with a house overrun with kids. Being decent parents hadn't come easily, and their efforts had long been forgotten under the notion that parenting skills were for the "high-class." Sadly, Ray had given up on his kids long before they had given up on him. The regular welfare money had come in quite handy, especially with Ray's unpredictable wages. Even then, between the booze, bingo, and groceries, it had become increasingly difficult to make ends meet and continue to stay under social services' radar.

With no place to go, Ray reluctantly moved, this time alone, into yet another shoebox-size tenement house. Nanny, always juggling a handful of various businesses at any one time, was currently trying to rent out to some unsuspecting fool a rundown fixer-upper without running water. Well, as luck would have it for Ray, his stay wouldn't be longstanding. By the second month, when Nanny had come by to collect the rent money, the stench from the house greeted her at the door. Between the rank urine smell and whatever the hell had crawled up in that place and died, she had all she could do not to vomit lunch all over the front steps. Eviction was getting more and more familiar to poor drunk Raymond.

"It wasn't much to look at, but neither was Ray." Clayton chuckled at his own quick wit, as he put the last nail into the shingles. In little less than an afternoon, Clayton and a mostly sober Ray had put the roof on his new living quarters. No bigger than a modern-day walk-in closet, Ray's new home peeked out of the tree line and lay flush with one of Clayton's oversized vegetable gardens. Home this go-round consisted of a twin bed, a couple of shelves on the wall, a small table, a chair, and a couple of dirty magazines. A modest bathroom was designated as a spot approximately six feet from the front door of his living space and was fully air conditioned, as it came without any walls. A five-gallon bucket to squat on and some soft dirt to catch his urine so it wouldn't splash back on him were good enough.

Running water wouldn't be necessary. Bathing had been one of those frivolous things, right up there with tea parties. It had been several years since Ray had violated a bar of soap, and he intended to keep it that way. Even his hands had remained quite parched for the better part of his adult life. Drinking water was provided by way of an old dirty blue water jug and drank reluctantly only after all twist-offs had been emptied.

Ray was an odd one. He was darker than most any man I had ever seen.

Clayton wouldn't have let coloreds in, so I knew he was a white man underneath all the dirt and tan. His hair was cut to within half an inch of his head and stood straight up like the vegetable brush Beatrice so loved to use to scrub the life and dirt out of our hair at the kitchen sink during our monthly hair washings.

Ray's teeth had seen better days, as they were mostly rotted down to nubs divided into mixed stages of decay. It was hard to imagine that a full set of white teeth had ever actually broken through Ray's filthy gums. He was short, thin, and wiry with a tattoo across his shoulder and one that ran horizontally on his forearm. In my limited experience, he seemed like an equal mixture of jailbird and drifter. In spite of his stench, Ray was kind and soft-spoken. He never became angry and out of control like Clayton. He hardly even flinched when Beatrice nicknamed him "pisspot."

Clayton liked having servant quarters in his backyard. Access to Ray would be day and night. After all, he paid him by the week, not by the hour.

Clayton figured that cutting Ray's weekly pay in half would be a good start to help pay for his generous living quarters. Ray would be Clayton's bitch, twenty-four/seven—a servant with a strong back and muscular arms to handle any grunt work both at home and in the woods. Clayton would now have full control of Ray, right down to when he could sleep. This new living arrangement would bring a lot of entertainment for Clayton.

Accommodations came complete with a three-hundred-foot extension cord that stretched through the rows of corn and beans, plugging neatly into a three-prong socket above the freezer sitting on Clayton's back porch.

This electrical umbilical cord kept Ray's comfort in the hands of Clayton exclusively. Lights had to be earned, not given without cost. Clayton practiced excessively for the first several months, with his unique form of Morse code. Power *off* had a couple of meanings. It was up to Ray to come down the field and check with Clayton whenever his lights were unplugged.

On each trip, he was instructed to find Clayton and gather his next set of instructions. *Off* always meant a trip through the field. The rest was up to Clayton. Sometimes, it was just a test, and other times, *off* meant it was time to work in the woods, the gardens, just about anything Clayton could think up.

Ray's place in our family would be a confusing one for several decades.

Sometimes, he was treated like Clayton's drinking buddy. It was after those binges that we were instructed to "load" Ray into the wheelbarrow and take him up through the gardens to his shack. Ray never owned a car, and he often referred to the wheelbarrow as his Cadillac. Other times, he was treated like livestock, beaten and kicked about unmercifully. Ray rarely complained, regardless of the dangers at any given moment.

Fortunately for Ray, his needs were few and gratitude somehow befuddled good common sense. As long as he could take comfort nursing his bottle to sleep each night, the rest of his worries wouldn't seem all that important.

Alcohol had pickled the common sense right out of poor, filthy Ray.

Chapter 36

BEDS AND BEETLES

The crib had served its purpose. Its wooden arms had cradled and protected me from outsiders as well as giving me a soft and separate place to rest. As my legs continued to grow, my toddlerhood requirements were soon replaced with the more active needs of a four-year-old child, a child who not only craved more mobility but, innately, had a deeper desire for further protection from the monsters above. After I learned how to lift my body up and over the top rails, the underbelly of the crib and the cold linoleum floor below became my new safe haven. Safely pressed against the back wall, I could no longer be easily reached. I knew what monster hands were capable of, I had watched them as they grabbed, hit, pushed, and choked the other children—those without places to hide.

Unfortunately, sooner than imagined, my beloved nest became too small, and regardless of how much I tried to tuck all of me within the eight-inch-high slot, I could no longer fit. It was time to say good-bye to sweet dreams and take my place in the monsters' world.

Beatrice sang under her breath as she made light work of the remaining legs of my wooden world, chopping them up for firewood. "No more babies in this house." She liked this new tune, she thought as she tossed the now kindling wood into the woodpile, the pile that would feed the indoor woodstoves in the months to come.

Thriftiness was paying off once again as the old crib mattress pad, salvaged from the woodpile, was placed on top of an old dilapidated dresser Beatrice had shoved up against the west wall of the girls' room. The paint was chipped and flaking off; most of its original white had been rubbed off into a less-attractive gray undercoat. My new bed had been a winning garage sale find.

Not accustomed to dangling so high from the floor, I knew one wrong turn would result in a dangerous tumble to the linoleum below. The bed was too narrow, so switching sides became a deliberate act, a process of jumping down from the dresser, turning to face a new direction, and then aligning my hands behind my back to assist in lifting myself up, butt-first, back to bed. Nothing was ever easy, and this was just more proof of that.

As spring set in, I was finally becoming better adjusted to my high-rise sleeping arrangements. Now able to sleep in one position for extended periods of time, I began to worry less about broken arms and legs. It just so happened that comfort would once again be short-lived. I was soon to realize that I wasn't the only living creature to find solace between the folds of my single sheet and the half a dozen mismatched blankets. A county's worth of black ground beetles had also been searching for higher ground since the spring rains. Colonies of hard-shelled insects had taken comfort under my pillow and everywhere blankets met blankets into dry little hiding places.

The first night that I met my new bedmates face-to-face, I was trying to fluff some life into my wafer-thin pillow. As I lifted it up from the mattress, hundreds of unsuspecting ground beetles, startled, began running in all directions for cover and a place to hide from the light.

Impulsively, a bloodcurdling scream escaped from my lips before I had a chance to think twice about what I had just done. My sisters' faces became pale, horror-stricken—not so much for the beetles now making the bedcovers quiver but for the storm I had likely just unleashed in the living room where Beatrice and Clayton sat watching the news.

Beatrice, in charge of the task of figuring out what the hell all the screaming was about, made her presence known as she stood with hands on hips in the doorway.

"Bugs, bugs, bugs," I whimpered as a steady stream of tears pooled into the neckline of my nightgown. Pointing in the direction of my makeshift bed, I knew it was either win Beatrice over fast or take a beating for my outburst.

The look on Beatrice's face was out of character and hard to read. A smile broke out on her face and quickly turned to laughter.

"Get back in bed and stop worrying about a few little bugs. They can't hurt you anyway. They are more afraid of you than you should be of them. Tomorrow we will see if there is a hole in the wall behind the dresser, and if so, we will put a rag in it." Beatrice found it quite comical to see her little Helen all in a tizzy over such nonsense. Beatrice really hated bugs, but as long as they stayed out of her bed, why bother with the task of getting rid of them, anyway?

That night's ordeal lasted throughout the rest of the spring and into the early summer months. The hole in the wall did lead directly outside, continuing to attract every black beetle in sight. Beatrice refused to let anyone block their path, as the game was too important to her. After all, it became a good source of entertainment and a bargaining chip whenever she wanted to further keep me in line.

"Someday, I will see about those bugs, if you are good."

The beetles, now accustomed to my scent, took over every dresser drawer as well as the bed I slept in. Lying awake each night, I would flail my arms, legs, and head in hopes that all the movement would encourage the bugs to become unsettled enough to leave for good.

Chapter 37

FOLLIES OF THE FRUIT

"Get your lazy ass up. I will bounce your head on the floor if you are not up and out of this goddamn bedroom in ten seconds." Clayton's drunken tenor resonated throughout the whole house and probably could be heard outdoors if there would have been any other houses within a mile or so of hearing distance.

The beetles and I had been in a deep state of slumber and were not prepared for our 2:00 a.m. awakening, even though we had been expecting it.

What started out as a once-a-week event had begun to turn into a more regular event, an "insanity after hours" party.

Like zombies, single-file, we shuffled out into the living room. The last couple of middle-of-the-night excursions had been a girls' only night out.

Tonight, however, Tony would be joining in on Clayton's fun, so unlucky for him. Tony had pissed off Clayton earlier in the day by being overheard telling Alice that he was better-looking than anyone in the house. Clayton took exception to it and wouldn't be upstaged by a boy who didn't look like his in the first place. Tony, even if he was only fifteen, was already strong enough to knock Clayton on his ass but always thought better of it.

Curtis had been exempt from the middle-of-the-night madness, as he had begun to show promise in the eyes of Clayton. Ever since Nanny had bought him that full-size piano, he was looking more like dollar signs every day. That kid could play anything capable of a tune. Throwing him an occasional free pass would pay off someday when Curtis made his place in the world of music. It would take a lot of that cash money to pay Clayton back for putting a roof over Curtis's head and putting up with his racket all these years. Curtis was going to be his savings bank.

Beatrice had been rubbing the sleep out of the corner of her eyes when she took a powerful punch from Clayton. She was always invited to the after-hours party, never knowing if she would be in the audience or one of the performers for the evening. The solid hit to her face was Clayton's way of reminding her that he had already told her once to go get an orange from the refrigerator.

"Grab a goddamn grapefruit too, you lazy bitch. For your disrespect, you will be rolling with your worthless kids tonight."

Clayton was never a man to ask for anything more than once, unless it had to do with filling a water glass with alcohol. It didn't matter if demands were said under his breath, fully knowing that the receiver couldn't hear them. It was not his responsibility to correctly deliver his message but the receiver's to get it right the first time.

Beatrice had earned a spot standing at one end of the metal kitchen table, as her short, thick legs weren't much for sitting on the floor. Tony stood at the opposite end of the table as if they were going to play Ping-Pong.

Beatrice and Tony began to push the grapefruit back and forth to each other along the slick metal table. Constantly in motion, they had much more at stake, as the sound made from a grapefruit hitting the floor made Clayton's neck snap over in the direction of the violation. A leather belt or an open hand, Clayton had his choice of tools to get everyone thinking straight.

Sitting spread-eagle on the living room floor seemed to be the best way to make sure the triangle of legs kept our orange in the playing field. The rules of the game were actually quite simple: keep the fruit in constant motion by rolling it to each player, clockwise if more than two players or simply back and forth if only two players. Stray fruit was a direct sign of disrespect and would cost us all dearly. If the fruit became motionless, that would be a penalty, a severe penalty. As with any game, all players had to remain enthusiastic and eager to continue playing. Often, the game would carry on until only minutes before the school bus was to arrive.

Tonight, Clayton would serenade us by strumming on his old broken-down guitar. Clayton couldn't make actual music come out of that acoustic box if he had rigged it up with a radio first. The offbeat, almost comical sound that came from his drunken strumming was our cue to sing, hum, just about any damn thing. It didn't matter what the song as long as we sang. In hindsight, singing was a good way to keep us awake and not risk falling asleep during "family night."

The first time I saw her at the bottom of the makeshift curtain that served as a door to the room I shared with Alice and Sadie, I had just taken a cuff to my right ear for not being a team player. It seemed that I had foolishly closed my eyes for a moment and my head had jerked noticeably when I regained my senses.

The nylon curtains slowly parted, forming a capital letter A about a foot off the floor. As if someone was lying on her belly, peering at us through the curtain, a figure appeared. Unfortunately, this person seemed to be missing her body from the waist down.

The old woman looked angry. Her stark white hair was pulled tightly into a bun pinned to the back of her head. Her eyes were cold, set deeply into the back of her sockets. With large, dark pupils, she looked frightening. Her mouth was puckered as if she had been sampling the grapefruit that was turning to juice on the kitchen table. A loosely crocheted shawl was draped over her shoulders, which she held tight with arms folded across her chest.

The fringe from the shawl blended into the floor and seemed to slightly flutter from the movement of air coming in from an open window. She continued to glare without speaking. I guess she didn't appreciate my nodding off either.

Fearing that I was somehow asleep, I turned away from the woman and started rolling with gusto, singing an old Loretta Lynn favorite of my mother's. Perhaps the song would serve a dual purpose and possibly score me some brownie points with Beatrice too. Now, feeling certain that I was really awake, I turned to look at the bottom of the curtains again. The woman's eyes met mine with her cold, intimidating glare. Had she been insulted that I had turned away? Was this someone else who would demand my respect, giving nothing in return?

For whatever reason, I was the only one who ever saw the old woman in the curtain. After the first few times of pointing toward the bottom of the curtains, trying to show Sadie something she could not see for herself, I gave up. There was always enough worry to go around, so I accepted that maybe the old woman was just my problem. I would continue to see her several more times over the course of our years of late-night craziness. Her expression never changed; she would stare for a few minutes and then would be gone until the next time.

The old woman was just the beginning. It was as if she were the master of ceremonies, the announcer of things to come. I knew that we were not alone in the house. It was difficult not knowing if this was a comforting turn of events or if in fact the other world that coexisted with us was much like Beatrice and Clayton. Was it a surreal world that somehow I had become a part of, leaving behind all the others? Yes, I would come to know the others who lived just beyond the curtain, whether I wanted to or not.

Chapter 38

DRIFTERS

There is not a king alive or dead who ever followed his own rules. At least that is what we were told when strangers started showing up at our house.

Clayton had become the pied piper of drifters, especially the thirsty ones.

Slick as an overnight ice storm, Clayton could charm the trust and common sense out of anything standing on two legs. With open arms, he would invite in whatever bum happened to be kicking up dust or sleet while passing by our dirt driveway.

Discreetly, Clayton referred to his friends as his pets. There was an odd mixture of nationalities, among them, an Irishman, Canadians, and some Mohawk Indians. As Beatrice was part Mohawk, boasting stories of a great-grandmother who actually sat around the fire smoking a peace pipe with her male counterparts, Mohawks were, as she put it, kinfolk.

Funny as it was, we were quick to find out that Clayton was actually afraid of the Indians. On a number of occasions after some home-spun fun, topped off with plenty of pure stilled grain alcohol, Clayton discovered that arm wrestling turned wild when losers pulled out hunting knives from their boots. Clayton eventually learned not to play cowboys and Indians with his braided-hair friends.

Clayton neatly categorized his pets into friendship longevity. Men with cars had a tendency to either become long-term friends or the ones who spun their tires out onto state tarmac after figuring out what kind of games Clayton liked to play. Men dependent on Clayton for a safe ride home became his favorites. Strays, as Clayton called them, were lost men with few family ties. These men were usually good, safe choices.

Being quite the host, Clayton provided his guests with an all-they-could-drink evening of fun. Sometimes the offerings became more extensive and included a tumble in the back bedroom with Beatrice, while Clayton watched. Rolling out the red carpet ensured that long-term friends kept coming to the party so when Clayton needed a favor, they would be hard-pressed to comply. The less-fortunate participants were in the short-lived friendships—men and even some women to be punished by night's end for not being able to resist the temptations put before them by Clayton and Beatrice.

"Weak fucking canaries and whores need to be taught a lesson."

Each lesson began the same, with advanced classes in drinking methodologies. No lesson was ever complete until Clayton hooked up his pressure cooker still, complete with copper tubing on the front gas burner of the kitchen stove. Drop by drop, the liquid devil flowed through elaborate tunnels, increasing in proof all the while. Pure grain alcohol could put a two-hundred-pound man on his ass with two or three shots and permanently bury a smaller man. Hard cider made a remarkable chaser, following the burn down through the gut.

Clayton had practiced enough with his "white lightning" that he could always hold a little more than his drinking partners. That came in handy when things had to be wrapped up and the rest of the night required a clearer head.

It was important that after a certain amount of drinking, playing the guitar, singing, and friendly arguing that Clayton shoo off any company who had vehicles. He would declare the night over for them, with a side wink to his remaining "best friend." The drunker the driver, the more fun the game to Clayton. As long as the man could start the car and press the gas pedal, Clayton figured God could sort out the rest.

"Better drive fast so you can beat the storm," Clayton said with a chuckle as he shut the car door behind his latest semiconscious victim.

The skies hadn't seen a lick of rain in several weeks, but a drunk man usually listens to "good" common sense at the worst of times.

The remaining, new best friend liked being the last guest at the party.

A dangerous feeling of confidence mixed with a deadly amount of cockiness ensured the last to leave would undoubtedly be the "never to leave" guest.

Leaving the party wasn't part of Clayton's grand finale. Alcohol has a way of loosening a man's tongue, causing him to act disrespectful with words he might not otherwise say. Loose lips were cause for Clayton to protect his home and his property from any foreseeable trouble. He knew that even lap dogs could be provoked if you squeezed them just right.

"A man's home is his castle, and he must protect it until death."

Hiding behind closed doors, bathed in sweat, we sat alone, completely terrified, pressing our ears to walls and looking for any movement coming from the outer side of the windowpane.

There was nothing to discuss. Despair came in the thickness of these nights and choked us of intelligible words. Why say out loud what we already knew, always knew. Talking made it too unbearably real. Clayton was a keeper. "Last to leave" wouldn't be going home that night or forever.

No free ride for a poor, stray drunk.

With muted shuffling, the cellar door opened. Hollow-sounding thuds could be heard as something heavy made contact with each cellar step.

That night's guest would remain on the wet cellar floor until morning when he would be laid to rest with Clayton's coyotes up on the hill.

The evening's horror show had finally come to an end.

"God, please protect me and keep me normal through this. Amen."

Chapter 39

ROMAN BATHS

Clayton felt rejuvenated. His past evening's entertainment had been an adrenaline rush. After a quick trip to the woods, dumping the body of his new best friend, he came back home to eat a solid breakfast and pick up Curtis, Tony, and Ray. On Saturdays, they would get in a little work before the noontime heat brought the deerflies out with a vengeance, then it would be quitting time for the weekend.

Saturdays were easy for him. Other than driving the tractor some, Clayton's work would be done before it got started. Wandering off to check the property lines was a Saturday task that ensured Clayton some quite time to reminisce and plan his next move. Clayton always felt at peace and more at home in the woods than anywhere else. People, including his own family, were a constant aggravation. Here, alone, a man could think without interruptions. A meal seemed like a simple gift he could provide to the animals that lived in his special place.

Curiosity would gnaw at him until he checked in to see if breakfast had been discovered yet. Coyotes have a sharp sense of smell. Clayton would be surprised if breakfast hadn't already been split up. It was a win-win situation for Clayton. He liked being clever, crafty, and smart. Winning had its own taste and its own melody. Clayton felt like a man on top, a very dangerous man on top.

The wood hooks, which were nothing more than tools of steel shaped in the letter C, complete with a filed-down tip, held together by a wooden handle, had already been unloaded by Ray along with the chainsaws. Hooks made loading the fifty-foot wooden giants a lot easier than palms and fingers. Curtis and Tony worked hard connecting hooks to wood butts and chains to bark, preparing the logs for their tractor ride through the skid way.

Tony had a wrestling match to prepare for and didn't want to waste valuable time taking water breaks. Curtis hated to sweat but knew that without his efforts going at least 80 percent, he wouldn't make it back in time to fire up his trumpet for the funeral he had agreed to play taps for.

Ray had already been working on the six-pack that he had hidden behind the chainsaw while loading up the truck. Ray didn't care much about time. Drinking in the woods or drinking in his shack, either way, his days were all the same anyway.

After a good sweaty morning in the woods, Saturday was the day Clayton cleaned up. It was an important event, as it signaled that the rest of us were going to get washed up too. With the bathroom now equipped with an actual flushable toilet, a person's business could be done without him or her having to leave the house. Unfortunately, it had been added to the big book of rules that the toilet was only to be flushed when it was completely full of shit, and toilet paper was never, ever to be flushed down with it. The septic tank cost money to empty, so flushing was done only with permission and inspection from Clayton. An old paper grocery bag sat within inches of the side of the toilet, a reminder that all toilet paper was to be deposited inside of it. The rule book stated that the bag had to be recycled until the bottom fell out, and only then could we have a brand-new paper bag to fill up.

The boys were allowed their own bathwater. It was understood that they could take baths and even fill up the tub about halfway. Men got dirty, and they were entitled to the water. Clayton turned bath day into a holiday and would head into the bathroom, shut the door, and be in there the better part of the afternoon. Only when done would he call Beatrice in, and it would be her turn to slip into the wash water and remove the scurf from the back of her knees and the rest of herself. She probably would have taken exception to sharing Clayton's bathwater had it not been for the simple fact that she was actually first in line for it.

Being the youngest and the last in line didn't come with much hope of taking off more dirt than I was preparing to have put on. Gray and dirty, the leftover water had a bar-soap sheen that glazed over its surface. Any warmth had disappeared long before it was my turn, and the dirt already on me seemed a whole lot healthier than the dirt staring back at me from that porcelain trough.

Once, I thought I had outsmarted Clayton and had run a short sink of water to take a sponge bath instead. Unfortunately, my timing had been awful, and when Beatrice came in to surprise me with her new Polaroid camera, she stumbled upon a less-than-naked girl, one with her feet hoisted up in the sink. *Ungrateful* was the only non-four-letter word I was called that unforgettable day. From that memorable experience, I learned to strip down, jump into the bathing mud puddle, and prepare for the bath police at any moment to come in and snap some black and whites as proof that I was complying with the rules.

Had we all been able to fit in the tub together, Clayton would have been a happier man. But without the means to widen the tub, the ingenious man had seen to it that no emotional rock had gone unturned. He had found a way to turn basic human needs into a twisted little game designed for his pleasure.

As he just fished out his upper and bottom plates from the jar still blue from its dose of Polident, Clayton's mouth had never felt a toothbrush. Saving all that money on toothbrushes and toothpaste had only helped him to buy his second set of false teeth, which he only wore for special occasions, namely Saturday nights. Shaving was the final order of business, and as inch-long whiskers stuck to the bowl of the aging sink, Clayton started looking like a handsome man—a very twisted yet handsome man.

A couple of slaps of Aqua Velva would do the trick, completing his once-a-week preening ritual.

Saturday nights were known as barroom nights for Clayton. As long as Beatrice hadn't pissed him off during the week, she was invited to come too.

Knowing that he was heading out to get drunk and dance with other women made Clayton generous and decent, however temporarily. We knew if there were a couple of gigantic-sized bags of barbecue potato chips and regular chips sitting out on the kitchen counter by afternoon, we were almost guaranteed a night free of Beatrice and Clayton's abuse.

Potato chips, in reality, were no more than bait, a small act of contrition by an evil mother and father. Sadly, it worked every single time. It didn't matter that we were alone, free from the two people who hurt us so badly. It was time that could have been better spent planning an escape or comparing notes at the very least. No, instead, we sat in front of the black-and-white television, scarfing down every last crumb of chips until our stomachs hurt and it was time to go to bed. We let opportunity pass us by, time after time.

Later, in the early-morning hours, loud drunken talk could be heard through the paper-thin walls. The bars had closed, and Beatrice, Clayton, and new best friend, female this time, could be heard laughing and cutting up in the living room. I got up and out of my bed quietly, so as not to alert anyone in the other room. Looking out the window, I was deeply relieved to see a strange vehicle parked in the yard. Tonight, I would sleep soundly. The boogeyman wasn't hunting tonight. As I pulled the blankets up and over my ears, trying to drown out the commotion a room over, I thanked God again, first for the potato chips and then for keeping me normal for yet another day.

Chapter 40

MYSTERY MEAT

Clayton manned the supper table like a guard at a maximum-security prison. With a thick leather belt in hand, he cruised the kitchen, lurking behind the chair backs of the five of us, encircling the tiny metal kitchen table we were all crammed around. Like duck, duck, goose, each and every time Clayton passed by our individual chairs, we had to take a bite of whatever it was that had ended up on our plates. Outside of the telltale vegetables, there was some serious concern even with the youngest of us that what we were eating wasn't meant for human consumption.

Beatrice was mainly in charge of cooking, although she was never much of a cook even on a good day. Most of her meals suffered a steam beating in her overused pressure cooker. Often, it became difficult to determine exactly what lay pulverized and jellied in between the mushy string beans or the wilted cabbage underneath boiled water. The only tradeoff with the meals cooked in steam was that whatever germs had originally been living off dinner were thoroughly sanitized and dead by the time they reached the table.

The only time Clayton got in the middle of what he deemed "women's work" was when he made his monthly kettle-of-soup surprise. Soup surprise was just that. No one ever really knew what was swimming in that pool of grease and tomato juice. Clayton would open the refrigerator, and whatever he saw, it went into the kettle—chocolate syrup, pancake syrup, ketchup, bologna, eggs, vegetables, old and new. Absolutely anything that caught his eye at that moment faced a watery death at the bottom of Clayton's soup kettle. Remarkably, a few of his creations were actually delicious. We never shared that information with him, as it would have only spoiled his fun with the supper-table game.

"Waste not, want not. Don't kill anything you won't eat. No store-bought food unless I tell you that you can eat it, and of course, eat what I goddamn give you." These mantras were recited over and over by a power-crazed, disturbed father.

Even as a youngster, I wondered if Canada knew that Clayton had been buying discounted horse meat from across their border, neatly wrapped in clear butcher paper. Galloping around the table, swinging the belt at us, was just plain evil, but it would make Clayton laugh and laugh to our detriment.

Horse meat became a regular staple at our table until it gained popularity and the price went up, relieving us of Clayton's pony show forever.

"Take a bite, goddamn it, or I'll shove your faces in it."

Roadkill was another favorite of Clayton's. Of course, he wouldn't eat it, but then again, he didn't have to. Raccoon, squirrel, rabbit—whatever ended up dead on the tarmac ended up on our plates. Boiled squid became a staple in our house off and on for a number of months. We were nowhere near an ocean. Clayton had found a little dank market that sold squid at deep discount prices. Dinner during squid fest turned into endless plates of snot-like piles of nasty, chewy, and flavorless creatures. Those nights always provided Clayton with an abundance of entertainment, as they were always good for a beating or two. Alice was known to pack a plate's worth of squid between her cheeks and still be able to talk through it.

"Swallow it fucking now, or I will beat the shit out of you." Clayton was all about choices.

Pork, chicken, fish, and the occasional beef were happy nights without need for beatings. Hungry and satisfied, we gobbled down every last hint of meat from those meals—happy times to wash away the pain and misery, allowing us to forget about the awfulness we experienced from just the meal before. Shortly after squid night became less exciting for Clayton, he brought home another mystery meat for supper. Beatrice had dutifully taken a break from the pressure cooker and as instructed had fried up slabs in a large cast-iron skillet, sprinkling them with various seasonings and a dusting of salt and pepper. Deer meat has a distinctive, tender, velvety flavor, so we knew it wasn't that, and bear season hadn't started yet. Large cuts of meat with a peculiar, sweet flavor. No one knew what to think of it. Dutifully, we ate it while Clayton looked on with fascination.

Mystery-meat nights were another way of controlling the children Clayton had so generously and unselfishly spared.

Chapter 41

BEAT TO THE HUM OF A DIFFERENT TUNE

Anger welled up inside of Alice. Betrayal lurked around every corner, hid behind every closed door, and stripped away any last shred of innocence.

Home became nothing more to Alice than a bad dream, with terrible images she could never wake up from.

She had always known that Beatrice resented her, despised her in fact.

Alice was brought home an angel, pure and innocent, and Beatrice couldn't bear to look at her. Competition wrapped in a receiving blanket. Alice would grow and blossom, in spite of the emptiness that would swallow her up most of time, swallow up us all. A beautiful musk rose with eyes the color of the sea and pain deep enough to drown in.

As she shivered in darkness, alone, perched on high rafters, her childhood progressed up and out of the attic. Where pain's reflection almost always stares back ugliness, the pain that welled up inside of Alice made her more irresistible to the treachery of Clayton. Alice became the damsel in distress with Clayton being the knight in shining armor. He was to rescue her from the wickedness of Beatrice and raise her stature above the rest of the family, all at a substantial cost.

Her arm in his, Clayton would parade his firstborn female down the dusty dirt road that lay behind the gardens, leading to nowhere in particular. He had one arm around Alice, the other around his flaccid Johnson, which lay exposed, resting on the outside of his unzipped fly. Behind the procession would be little Sadie, too young to understand but clever enough to know evil when she saw it. Beatrice came along, waiting and watching for the moment that Alice was least protected, waiting to strike out like a rabid dog, yet patient enough to wait for the right time to administer a lethal dose of payback.

Crazy like a fox was growing sharp, dangerous fangs.

As Alice's body started changing, evolving into that of a young woman, menstrual cycles became part of her changing new world. Beatrice waited until she could smell blood each month before she ripped the clothes off from Alice's back and swung her blood-soaked panties in the air like a flag of victory. Cruelly, Beatrice would demand that Alice stand naked in front of us so we could see what a whore looked like. Alice held her head high during her abuse, even though her body quivered with fear and shame. It wasn't her fault that she bled.

After one particularly damaging afternoon alone with Beatrice, Alice lost against her own inner restraint and set about unleashing her bottled-up rage, which couldn't be squelched any longer. Ripping and tearing at her own skin, Alice dragged her fingernails first horizontally and then vertically, raking them deep into her beautiful skin, leaving angry red streaks that sent droplets of blood drizzling all over her naked body. She would show Beatrice firsthand, creating a brutal, visual picture of what emotional abuse looked like when the mind simply could not hide it anymore.

Physical abuse has a way of staring right back at you, making it hard to turn a blind eye to it. Beatrice knew Clayton would be furious with her and would not believe it when she told him that she did not put the scratches on Alice. It would look to Clayton like Beatrice had broken the rules, had been a disobedient wife. Alice was not to be damaged goods unless Clayton was the one in charge of the damaging. With her heart racing in her chest, Beatrice waited, knowing full well when Clayton walked through the front door all hell would break loose. Beatrice was bracing herself for a hellacious beating.

The hum began as a way to bring relief, to settle the nerves and diffuse the trouble. Alice could feel it resonating in her throat as she tried to drown out the sound from the beating Beatrice was receiving at the hand of Clayton for defacing his property. She had taken enough abuse of her own; it was hard to feel remorse for Beatrice. The humming grew inside of Alice, becoming louder and louder. Its tone marked the dawning of newly found control. Finally, the sense of power that had been buried deep, had abandoned her until then, returned. If she had to endure life under Clayton, then why not share the misery and burden with the mother who tortured her as well?

Clayton heard the humming coming from the kitchen. He recognized it as the voice of his oldest daughter. He liked the fact that Alice could find enjoyment in one of his favorite activities. He would let her know when he was done with Beatrice that he enjoyed her music and would look forward to hearing it again soon.

Indeed, as Clayton had wished, he would hear his daughter's signature hum again, calling to him, signaling to him that Beatrice needed reckoning with. The emotional war between the three of them had taken an ugly, destructive turn. This time, Alice had the upper hand.

Alice as new head queen took authority over Sadie and me. With most of her focus on Sadie, Alice ruled with an iron fist, capturing all the hatred that Clayton had taught her. Allies no more, the next several years of our lives would be spent caught up in a vicious power struggle between three people not to be crossed—Clayton, Beatrice, and a very angry Alice. Despair, partnered with power, created a lethal combination, causing our world to become even more unstable. One of our own had crossed to the other side, swallowed up in a fit of rage.

Chapter 42

BLACKBIRD

Take these broken wings and learn to fly.
—the Beatles

The room had just gotten tossed, which simply meant that Clayton felt that one of us had neglected to make him feel special. Clayton had diffused his anger by having a man-sized temper tantrum that had spun out of control in our bedroom.

Beatrice also had a habit of tossing our room whenever clothes were not properly folded and put away. Those episodes usually resulted in everything we owned that resembled laundry, including bedding, being tossed into a pile in the middle of the room. A "surprise" for the kids to find when they came home from school. This had not been her work, as the latest surprise included overturned furniture, a trademark of Clayton's handiwork.

Clayton had exercised his rage sufficiently and didn't feel it necessary to continue with his tirades when the school bus came to a stop in front of our house. One look around revealed the upheaval—just another day in paradise.

After the usual chores and between the business of making, eating, and cleaning up dinner, the room got put back together, quickly and quietly.

Again, we had lived through another episode of "puzzle night" in the Clayton household, with all five hundred pieces being flung in different directions in our tiny bedroom.

Bedtime was determined by the season. During the summer months, we had a few extra hours of daylight in which we could be outside, away from Clayton and Beatrice. Although we couldn't go far, it was empowering to feel the night air, the evening breeze, for a couple of sacred hours.

Wintertime not only brought with it limited daylight hours, but an overwhelming feeling of hopelessness. With bedtime shortly after the last of the supper dishes were dried and put away, it was increasingly difficult not to feel claustrophobic when five o'clock came and the outside was cloaked in total darkness. Bedtime came when darkness arrived, whatever time that might be. It was just the way it was; the rule book required it.

"Lights out" always came as a mixed blessing. It wasn't easy to determine which nights would end up as family night, rolling oranges and grapefruits until the early morning hours. With so much uncertainty as to what the night might bring, it was always best to attempt as much sleep as we could whenever we were allowed to be in our room.

Sleep, however needed, was tricky business for me. The beetles had moved on, but the restlessness that had come with them had not left.

Sleepwalking was scary business, especially for a young child who was already very afraid of the dark, along with a multitude of other things.

Regardless of many internal fears, a couple of times a week, I would somehow navigate my way off the dresser and walk down the hall and out the back door, which led to complete darkness. The night usually played out in the same manner, nearly every time. Eventually, the sounds coming from the cornfields of coy dogs running between the rows of cornstalks out on their evening hunt for small prey, would bring me out of my sleep-induced late-night walk. Terrified and dazed, I would hightail it back up the steps and to my bed, more afraid to be caught by Beatrice and Clayton than by any coy dog.

Coy dogs were bizarre creatures, nocturnal and chatty, a hybrid offspring of a coyote and a dog with the most incredible, distinctive howl you will ever hear. Their young tend to have a youthful, high-pitched howl and when mixed with the tenor of the older males, it is a noise straight from a Halloween soundtrack.

When I wasn't wandering out in the middle of the night, I began to experience intense night terrors. Everything awful during the day began to replay itself in my dreams each night. Unfortunately, it felt even more vividly real, more painful than I allowed myself to feel during the actual event. Sadie was the first to realize that letting me scream it out in the safety of the backseat of the rusted-out station wagon with the windows tightly rolled up was the smartest choice. She would stay with me, however long it took, until deep sleep replaced the screaming. Sadie knew full well that this type of disobedience would have severe consequences if and when Beatrice and Clayton ever found out. Sadie was always careful to bring me inside before morning and before our absence was discovered.

Since my first introduction to the old woman in the curtain, I had begun to have a heightened sense of awareness. In the limited capacity of a first-grader, I was beginning to see, feel, and hear stuff that I hadn't before.

Had I known that these extended senses were not natural, I would have been very frightened by them. I didn't know until years later that most people only saw darkness when they shut their eyes, not another view. I soon learned that if I relaxed my breathing and closed my eyes, I could locate my father clearly and colorfully in my head. With practice, I learned how to almost wear him like a coat, giving me the advantage of knowing where he was and what he was doing. This new gift spared me several beatings, as it became my breath, my existence to remain one step ahead of him.

Unfortunately, nothing comes without cost, and at times, what I would see him doing behind closed eyes was beyond horrible—terrible and awful things that stayed trapped in my own head, unable to get out.

Time was to be my only relief. I would grow up, leave the house, and simply be normal. I had prayed nearly every day to God, and I wouldn't stop until I was sure no matter what happened, I would be normal. Life had been a sacrifice, and my one request was to let me leave here fully emotionally intact.

When I closed my eyes for the night, time faded off into an enormous garden with rows stretching to heaven. I had a lot of work that needed to be done. A long stretch to hoe for a small girl. I had lived through another night of screams and torment. Would restful sleep find me now?

They say that nirvana means something different to everyone. It would be many years before I would adequately give a name to the experience that found me that night. Out of character, instead of collapsing into an exhausted sleep, I fell into the most unbelievable dream, an experience and journey that would come gently for me whenever I needed it most, beginning then and for the rest of my life's stay.

As best as I can explain it, an indescribable feeling of light and warmth entered my body. The light was a brilliant white—not the kind of light that makes you squint but the kind that draws you nearer and nearer until you are the light, not just surrounded by it. Without thought, my body gently lifted up and off the bed. There were no walls, no windows, no rules, no restrictions. As I floated up and into the clouds, there was no worry, no pain, no remorse, no sadness, and no fear. The light lifted me up and held me in its arms, and we both flew through the air, through time, to places where white doves cooed on rooftops and gentle breezes caught leaves high up in the trees. Love wasn't a direction or goal but a gift that engulfed me without question, simply requiring nothing in return. My breathing resonated in my chest like the hum of energy, keeping me afloat, lifting me out of reach, out of pain, out of distance of my broken world. Faith was holding my fragile spirit in the palm of its hand.

Chapter 43

BROOMS AND DUST MOPS, A SUMMER BREAK

"Have you been shook yet?" Clayton took delight in his ridiculous morning ritual. Each morning started with an official "Get your ass out of bed," followed shortly by, "Have you been shook yet?" On most days, Clayton's presence in our doorways began between five-thirty and six.

This was our one opportunity to rise without getting our heads thumped onto the floor.

He took great pleasure in doing a temperament check by threatening a good shoulder shaking if our response didn't come across pleasant enough.

"Yes, sir, but I'll take another"—textbook answer to a question that really made absolutely no sense but generally followed a bad, naughty Clayton from the night before. He made temperament checks because while Clayton didn't tolerate laughter, he most definitely didn't tolerate sad or angry faces either.

A good, hard shake and our clocks were reset, ready to take on the day.

Occasionally, a grumpy Alice dared not respond and she would take an extra hard shaking to yank her back on track.

Summertime was in full swing, which meant only two things, full-time garden work and at least one week for me, two weeks for the older girls, at Nanny's house. Summer break was a privileged affair that came with state-of-the-art dust mops and brooms. Spring-cleaning had been renamed summer vacation by dear sweet grandmother. Nanny had a three-story mansion that was wedged between likeable city neighbors. With actual streetlamps glowing through the upstairs windows at night, her home felt safe and watched over.

Nanny didn't like dirt almost as much as she didn't like cleaning it up.

Our presence was an important part of her summer, as she knew her wooden floors would get a good solid waxing and her white walls would shine. By vacation's end, everything in her house would either be washed, dusted, polished, waxed, or vacuumed. In return, she would feed us, let us sleep in her soft featherbeds upstairs, and possibly thrust a dollar or two in our pockets for Saturday night bingo. Nanny made sure that any money she gave us, even if it was only a nickel, came with the order of "Don't tell anyone I gave you money to do your job." Yes, Nanny had found her Cinderella, in fact three of them, and she played the role of angry, mean stepmother very, very well.

Nanny had lost her sense of smell one day when she had toppled over the back of a kitchen chair. Rumor had it that she had been inspecting the top of the refrigerator for dust and had gotten overzealous in her reach. In the end, she had sought justice for her tragedy by finding ways to practically poison her grandchildren in the kitchen under the innocence of "not being able to smell if food was spoiled or not."

Meals were like peaches, covered in a thick, hairy overcoat that had to be peeled off before consuming. Somehow it had made sense to her that spoiled food could be eaten by children on account of their strong immune systems.

Curtis had been visiting Nanny quite a bit early one summer and had much enjoyed being coddled by a doting grandmother. It wouldn't have been so bad, but Curtis thoroughly enjoyed looking down his nose at the rest of us, pointing to his latest gift, new shoes from Nanny. Scrubbed and pristine, he hated to admit that he was related to the rest of us, dressed as we were, rejects from an outdated rummage sale. The honeymoon was almost over, however, and Nanny would be taking Curtis along with several bags of new clothes home.

Before she dropped off her first grandson, she felt it only right to take him out to a nice supper in a real sit-down restaurant. As an afterthought, she pointed to an opened can of spaghetti tinged the color green in the refrigerator.

"Heat that up for your dinner. Don't forget to wash the dishes afterward."

After scraping away the mold, we each took a tablespoon's worth of cold spaghetti out of the can and ate it silently over the sink. Yes, dinner had been served, and it was time to get to work. Nanny always adhered to Clayton's pink and ruthless rules.

Chapter 44

SINK OR SWIM

After a long week of bleach and Comet, I was ready to get back home and trade my mop in for a garden hoe. Beatrice and Clayton felt the same way and chided me for neglecting my chores at home while I was out gallivanting with Nanny.

Any child should know that responsibilities at home should always take precedence over city slicking with relatives. After all, the weeds had missed me. Alice and Sadie had another glorious week left to spend with grandmother, a.k.a. the evil stepmother, so the women's work at home needed immediate attention.

The rows were set up in the garden such that each one took approximately three hours to go from one end to the other. Hoeing and weeding were to be done correctly. On inspection, we didn't get any do-overs. Fortunately, Clayton had not been thinking "Clayton clear" when he had positioned the beehives and boxes a good distance away from the rows of vegetables.

Honeybees pollinated plants and produced honey. An accidental gift of being a good distance apart ensured relief from a constant agitation by honeybees while hoeing.

Even though Clayton was deathly allergic to a bee sting, that didn't stop him from having at least four or five active hives going at all times. He had Ray and the women to tend to the hives and strip them of honeycombs when the season permitted. A good summer was measured in how few bee stings I would receive while working out of doors. The average summer usually netted at least a half a dozen. This year, I was hoping to hit a new average, preferably lowering the number to none.

Garden spiders were everywhere and made such an impression on me that some of the screaming in the back of the station wagon was on account of finding one crawling on my leg that very same day. Garden spiders are awful things. With thick, large bodies of bright yellow and black, their legs long and creepy would spin their webs throughout the tomato and potato plants and wherever else they felt like it. I have never actually been bitten by one, nor have I ever heard of anyone receiving a nasty bite from one either, but nevertheless, between Sadie and me, we were most certain that one day we would end up stuck in their webs with a zillion of them closing in for the kill. Garden spiders were killers compared to my innocuous little friends, the black beetles.

Because our home and the two acres surrounding it had basically been cut out of the center of the woods, it wasn't uncommon to stumble on an occasional fox or wild dog cutting across our gardens, heading for less populated areas. Another cut into the woods had produced a less than savory bunch of skid-row type people who had shacks and starving dogs a couple miles east of our not-much-better-looking shack. Occasionally, their malnourished mutts would come around, sniffing for food and willing to fight for it too. I learned quickly and precisely how many steps it would take to cross the garden and leap onto the back porch in the nick of time.

Stray, mean, and vicious dogs and garden spiders were my outdoor nemeses.

With the summer heat warming his backside, Clayton walked through the rows of produce, inspecting my progress along the way. The thermometer was hitting peak summer weather, and Clayton didn't enjoy being out of doors unless he had to. Working in the garden was thirsty work. Him bringing a water jug outside to share hadn't crossed either of our minds. I suspected that Clayton would have brought one for himself had he planned on spending any quality time under the sun. For now, he was just fine watching his daughter working up a heated sweat.

"Sure would be nice to be out at the lake right now …" Clayton paused for effect. "Do a little fishing and maybe some swimming too? A person would be able to cool right off if they were floating right out there on that big lake."

Clayton held his hand high as if he were painting the ripples on the water's surface in the air surrounding him. "Maybe you could come along this time, seeing the boys are off working their summer jobs and your sisters are running the roads with your grandmother."

Clayton owned a rowboat that he had rigged up to a good-size motor.

Once or twice a year, he would load it up, unplug Ray's electricity, signaling him to get down to the house, and the two of them would head off to the lake with fishing poles. Ray didn't seem to enjoy their little excursions to the lake and usually had an odd expression on his face that I could see through the windshield of the truck as Clayton was backing out onto the road with boat in tow.

Having never seen a lake, I found it hard to imagine all that water in one place. Curtis and Tony had been allowed to take up swimming lessons a couple of summers back, but girls didn't need to know how to swim so Alice, Sadie, and I hadn't spent any real time around water outside of the water that collected down in the cellar every spring.

Clayton had never paid much attention to me unless he wanted something.

Maybe he needed someone to cast an extra line out or maybe even shove the boat out until it caught hold with the current. It didn't matter if I had to carry the boat over my head all the way to the lake, I was being asked to join along for company. Maybe there was a side of Dad that could be nice when he wanted to. After all, I knew it took a lot of effort to be the boogeyman; maybe even he needed a break from time to time.

Ray didn't need a signal to come down to the house, as he had already been on his way, hoping to find a little afternoon dinner in the process.

Alcohol fueled his tank, but food was the oil in his engine. It didn't take much to keep it running, just enough to keep him upright during the day.

Clayton instructed Ray to get the boat ready and gas up the motor. He chuckled as he told Ray that I was going to come out to the lake with them.

Ray's jaw fell as he shot me a look of fear, a look I'll never forget.

Something was wrong, yes, very wrong.

I never let on that Ray had been the one to change my mind, that he had been the one to forewarn me, possibly saving my life while putting his at risk. Even in all his drunkenness, he had managed to do the right thing, the decent thing. He protected me even if it might cost him a tumble out of the boat if Clayton caught on to his loose lips.

Somewhat disappointed, Clayton accepted the excuse that I didn't feel right leaving all the work undone. Being on vacation had made me neglect my duties at home, and I would feel better if I tended to my responsibilities and maybe go out the next time.

As I settled back on my hoe under the noon-hour sun, tears streamed down my cheeks, leaving muddy trails that trickled down my arms onto the long wooden handle of my hoe. I had waited until the truck had been gone for a few minutes before the pain that welled inside of me cut loose. Ray might have been a drunk, he may have deserted his own family, but for this moment, he probably saved my life. Turns out Clayton wanted to play a little game with his youngest daughter—a game he lovingly referred to as "sink or swim." The game was played out in the center of the lake without a life vest. The rules were quite simple; players were shoved off the side of the boat. The winner would swim back to the boat, and the losers would simply sink until they drowned.

Firm ground under my feet, I was alone in my thoughts and confined to the gardens, the only place where I felt safe, where the birds sang overhead and my anger and sorrow could be beaten out of the weeds with a garden hoe, where honeybees pollinated the plants and my summer count had just increased by one.

Chapter 45

A RUSE

Some Christians use the Bible much as a drunk does a
lamppost—more for support than for illumination.
—Rev. William Sloane Coffin, quoted by H. Irvin Smith

I have always thought that if God would have come down from the heavens
and seen the shrine that Beatrice and Clayton had built in their bedroom
for his namesake, he probably would have lit them both on fire and then
handed each of us a stick of chocolate and a couple of marshmallows for
roasting.

Beatrice, being the good Catholic that she was, bought out Woolworths
and all of the other local five-and-dime stores of religious statues. Any
size, any make, Jesus, Mary, Paul, Matthew, and any other saint who had
a price sticker rendering him or her for sale, they all made their way home
with Beatrice.

Beatrice believed that she was creating her own little army of saviors, who,
with their presence alone, would wipe her slate clean. If nothing else, it
gave her a place to genuflect whenever she hadn't made the sign of the
cross nearly enough for one day. Beatrice was creating her own little City
of Babylon right in her bedroom.

Among the slew of statues that covered every nook and cranny of Beatrice's
dresser and shelves, there stood a picture of Jesus that became Beatrice's

favorite icon of our Lord. Encased in a cheap plastic twelve-by-fourteen-inch frame, Jesus smiled down at us every day. Beatrice wanted to make sure that Jesus had a good eye on us as she set about moving his picture from the walls of the living room to her bedroom walls and back again, over and over. In the picture, enrobed in long, flowing, illuminating brown hair, Jesus watched over us. His heart, depicted as the kind you find in a science lab and not the kind in a sweet valentine's card, lay exposed and wrapped in thorns.

Beatrice's framed Jesus didn't move me quite the same way it moved her.

I was terrified of the picture and did what I could to avoid its stare. This was not the Jesus that I knew; this was Beatrice's Jesus.

I had been taught how to kneel and how to ask for forgiveness right along with my brothers and sisters. None of us would be without Jesus whenever Clayton felt it was time for us to put a good word in for him. Just like those before me, I would confess my sins to the nuns and priest and receive first Communion before the year was out. Then seeking further instruction, someday with certificate in hand, I would be delivered and officially confirmed a child of God, qualified and willing to save those sinners put before me. Confirmation would be several years off, as I still had a distance to go before Clayton would consider me saving material anyway.

It wasn't long before Clayton made the decision that Jesus could come to our house instead of us going into town to see him at church. They were still on friendly terms, but Sundays were starting to aggravate Clayton. Besides the fact that the preacher had gotten stuck on the Ten Commandments the past couple of sermons, with a special emphasize on the sixth one, "Thou shall not kill," it seemed no matter where the Clayton clan sat on the back row of pews, Clayton, alpha male, with his legs splayed a good distance apart, the priest seemed to be looking right over at the sorry bunch of us.

Clayton hated small talk and did his best to clear out of the building before the priest made his way to the exit to shake each of our hands and ask if we had tithed. I, for one, knew that the handful of change that had been given to my oldest siblings had seen its way to the inside of their pockets just at the last possible second before the metal dish was passed. Maybe they were saving up for bus fare away from this farce.

It never made any sense how all these God-fearing church people never once tried to help. Through my eyes, it was more than obvious that Beatrice was taking a regular beating, as her bruises were always in a multitude of healing stages. So strange a group of good Christian people couldn't be bothered by a devil in their own backyard. Even when I motioned with my eyes for them to take a good look at us, they would smile sweetly, quietly, and quickly turn away—turning away from the whole reason they were there in the first place. Their backs and their neglect never quite made it to my heart for forgiveness, not now and probably never.

Even a seven-year-old knows when she is being shunned and dismissed by the Almighty's people.

Clayton could turn his faith on and off like a water faucet, especially when things didn't go exactly and according to his way of thinking. The weather was a good example of this and became an accurate barometer as to whether or not Clayton would be shaking his fist toward the heavens from the living room ceiling, shouting out blasphemous remarks, or whether he would be praising Jesus with bent knees, palms up, for another brilliant day in Clayton paradise. Yes, with the erratic North Country weather, Jesus and Clayton had a lot to talk about.

Months after we had settled into our own Sunday services governed by Clayton, he came home early from working in the woods in a feverish panic.

Crying, shaking, with the pallor of his face hidden behind a wall of sweat and fear, he could barely get the words out, stammering words that sounded much like a telegraph message: Jesus was pissed and was coming after him. Clayton paced the living room, looking out the windows as he spoke. I guess he thought that Jesus would drive up and park in the yard with a couple of angels in the backseat as backup.

The nun had warned him, even had felt sorry for him, Clayton ranted on.

As he spoke, his hands began to twist off the cap from a quart bottle of brandy. Two good swallows would right him enough to tell Beatrice exactly what had just happened. Continuing on, it seems that while taking a short water break out in the clearing, Clayton had looked up at the sky while tipping the water jug up to his mouth. Out of the corner of one eye, he saw an unbelievable sight coming from the heavens, making its way downward past the tree line. Parting the limbs as if on cue, a team of black horses being driven by a nun came out of the sky and skidded to a complete stop in front of Clayton.

Being God-fearing and all, Clayton immediately dropped to his knees as the nun approached him. Laying her hands on the top of his head, she started praying for his salvation. After a few moments of praying in tongues, she got back on her wagon with her team of horses and flew back toward the heavens, disappearing out of sight. Temporarily left blinded, Clayton had crawled around on the forest floor, begging a drink of water from Ray, who had supposedly seen the whole thing.

Clayton's thirst was building as his body became weak from all of the emotional excitement, drained from the power of his own story. Beatrice poured him a tall water tumbler of brandy to help take the edge off. She had heard enough of his nonsense and saw her opportunity to add a couple of the foil-wrapped sleeping pills that were snug inside her apron. The pills would fizz down to nothing before he would tilt back the brandy, never being the wiser.

"Let the fool sleep for a while," she murmured under her breath, wearing her crooked smile, which quickly turned to a caring, warm, thoughtful look as she turned toward Clayton. A nightie nightcap courtesy of a loving wife.

Nuns, true or not, would be just a memory by morning.

Later that night, while Clayton slept like the dead, Beatrice sat up in her chair, deep in thought, methodically tugging on single strands of her hair as she stared off into the distance.

I was very curious about Clayton's vision and probably a little hopeful too. I had seen my share of strange occurrences behind my eyelids so I wasn't quite ready to dismiss Clayton's experience as a mental breakdown. Maybe he had actually been a witness to some kind of spiritual revelation?

"So, do you think a nun came down from the heavens to pray over Dad?" I asked quietly, not wanting to startle her with my presence.

"Of course I do," Beatrice slowly said, turning to the sound of my voice. "Do you know why I know it is true, Helen?" Beatrice tilted her head so it was in line with mine, eyes meeting my own. "You must never tell anyone of our sins, Helen, but your father is the devil sent up from hell. We live with the devil here on earth because you kids have been such terribly bad sinners. It is our penance to suffer under the devil's wrath, our life burden, our ball and chain. Dear, don't ever forget you are the devil's offspring." Beatrice's words trailed off as she went back to her business of single strand hairs and staring into darkness.

The meaning of those words stung deeply. I knew they would replay over and over again as background noise in the inevitable nightmares that would come to chase me that night. Screaming was a natural product of tortured sleep. I would have to wake Sadie up to accompany me. She would understand; she always did. I needed the safety of the old car, where my screams would be out of ear's reach, spent out in the protection of the backseat. With another night of nightmares to endure, sunrise would be a long time coming.

Chapter 46

MUSIC MAN, THE LAST POST

Summer was coming to a close, vacations at Nanny's house were over, and each of us had survived another round of seasons, surprisingly enough.

School was soon to be back in full swing, essays due about what we did on summer break. Really, were they kidding? Surely, death, murder, mayhem, and of course finding out my father was the devil should net me an A or at the very least, three square meals in foster care. Instead, I played outside, blah, blah, and blah.

Curtis was officially a man now, according to the fine print typed on the bottom of his gold-foiled high school diploma. He had come to his adolescent finish line and now had other decisions to make. Either stay home, forever bound in his Stockholm headlock, or use his unprecedented talents in music to help create miles in distance and emotion.

Music had been everything to Curtis. Privileged in many ways, he could pick up a tune and play it on any instrument at his disposal. Curtis had an incredible ear for music and could have easily played rhapsody on a simple pair of kitchen spoons. His music teacher and his only true role model adored him, setting Curtis up with a multitude of opportunities to earn a little extra spending money and to further his love for music and melody. Curtis played at several military funerals, music played not so much for the living but as a final serenade and farewell to the dead. Curtis, with closed eyes, could play the most beautiful rendition of "Taps" anyone had ever caressed out of a trumpet.

With an overabundance of musical talents waiting to be discovered, Curtis was encouraged to apply for a spot on the local talent show that was broadcast live for television. His music teacher helped him fill out the paperwork and was jubilant when Curtis was chosen to play a formidable piece on the piano in front of a live audience. In the glow of camera lights, with opportunity waiting with open arms, Curtis froze, unable to play. The dead had not judged him or stared upon him, waiting for the wrong note to ring out above the others. Too nervous and paralyzed, Curtis sat on his bench, crushed for the whole world to see while he waited for the cameras to release their cold stare on him.

Curtis's music was a canvas of his life—words he could have never expressed out loud, melodies drenched in emotion and cloaked in a sadness giving listening ears time to reflect. Rich with sentiment, Curtis felt each chord he played, and it was how he related to the world around him. Missing his moment of fame and glory should have been expected. A lifetime of ugliness had been there to swallow him up, even when he tried to remove himself from it. Putting a dividing line between him and the rest of us had worked only on the surface. He had done his best to disassociate with his past, his siblings, and all that represented his poor, white-trash upbringing, only to find us tossed about in his head when he so much needed to think clearly.

Curtis had been given many privileges not afforded to his brother and sisters, but he too had suffered greatly under Clayton's wrath. Clayton's evilness had not spared Curtis even though the bulk of his abuse had been more mental. As a boy, Curtis had stood on the other side of drawn shades, numb and removed, while his sisters were raped and molested just feet away, separated by a thin windowpane. Even as he grew into a young man with strong arms, he continued to take refuge safely apart on the opposite side, tucked away in his separate world where heartache didn't exist and his worth wasn't measured in beatings.

We were an embarrassment to Curtis as he walked ahead of us, hoping that people would not conclude we were with him. Special meals, milk labeled "Curtis milk," sat on the top, front shelf in the refrigerator. He was better than us but cut from the same worn cloth and capable of feeling and remembering everything or nothing, all at the same time. He too was stuck in idle while the rest of the world moved forward.

The mailman had actually delivered the letter several weeks earlier. Beatrice had conveniently hidden it between the mountains of women's magazines that lined the side of her chair. Hoping to leverage some benefit out of its contents, she had held on to the letter, waiting for the right time to give Curtis the good news. A ride into town in Curtis's newly purchased used Ford Falcon seemed as good a time as any.

Curtis had forgotten that he had applied to various colleges, hoping to find one that would nurture his love for music. With virtually no money for college, furthering his education wasn't something he held high hopes for.

As he unfolded the single-page letter, a surge of hope hit him. Curtis had received a full scholarship to Fredonia State. Music man was getting an education and a chance at a new life.

Curtis was packed and ready to go by the end of the week. Beatrice was relieved that there would be less laundry to do on the wringer washer and one less mouth to feed. Clayton, however, had recognized that one of his soldiers was going AWOL. He felt slighted and angry that Curtis would want to leave his post to go to some goddamn college. Clayton took it as a personal insult that Curtis wanted to live his own life.

The tension in the house became thick with a mixture of anger, excitement, anticipation, and a feeling of downright anxiousness. No one had ever left the house before. As the youngest sibling, I hadn't sorted it all out that one could actually live long enough to grow up and leave the house forever. There was hope to wait for and time to pass. I was glad that we were one less in our house, as it made the journey not such an unreachable thing.

The day Curtis officially pulled out of the driveway with his backseat filled with all of his worldly possessions, I had been working in the garden, hoeing rows of potato plants. Coming into the house, I looked around and didn't see Curtis in the living room. Surely I could see him to say good-bye?

"Where is Curtis?" I asked Clayton, hoping for a less than emotional response.

Clayton looked at me with disdain chiseled into his face. "Forget about him. He is dead to us now."

The words hit me as I tried to sort out the real meaning of Clayton's hatefulness. Nevertheless, I couldn't shake the image of my oldest brother lying dead with someone playing a trumpet over him. I didn't really think that he had died but maybe had just forgotten to say good-bye and left for his new life. One thing was for certain; he was gone for however long gone was.

Had I been able to see Curtis more clearly when I closed my eyelids and traveled to the places most people never get to experience, maybe I would have chosen to get to know him better as I grew up.

Music man never finished college at Fredonia State. His music was laid aside for other pursuits, including marriages, children, and jobs that were beneath him. Occasionally, I heard that he would play his beautiful music on his guitar, which more often than not, sat abandoned in a closet. A time or two, he had played piano for his friends and new family. I never really got to see him much when he was all grown up, a man. Somewhere along the way, we let go of each other's hand and drifted far apart from each other.

Curtis loved what he loved and felt the world in ways that few could know or understand. His music stayed safely tucked in his head, its rich chords resonating behind his sad eyes, the eyes that sooner than later, I would never see again. Curtis passed away one day in his midfifties. A life cut short, a song unfinished. Perhaps he traveled in his afterlife to where clouds glide effortlessly over the horizon and music flows between the strings of an angel's harp. I can only hope that when the song faded out, he had found his peace.

KCT 1952–2009

Chapter 47

CRY FOUL AND CHEW LIKE A MAN

"Get your ass up now! Chickens don't pluck themselves!" Beatrice hollered from the kitchen.

Weekend mornings were usually full of adventure with time always set aside for family bonding around the kitchen table. Five o'clock came early to most folks; to us, it was just the start of another long weekend. In a farming community like ours, most folks owned high-dollar heifers and seeded countless acres of land to harvest for corn and grain. Our swampy lot held a poor man's crop, complete with a gross of chickens and roosters, the latter taking delight in chasing us around the yard, wielding their spurs and sharp talons, occasionally making a direct hit with the soft flesh of unsuspecting calves or a not so lucky gluteus maximus. The only other livestock outside of our feathered friends were a couple of fattened hogs behind an electric fence buying time until slaughter, come cooler weather.

Clayton had been outside shortly before dawn with his ax in hand, eager to start with his killing spree. It would take approximately thirty minutes to round up a dozen or more hens, the unlucky ones wouldn't be filling up on a belly of grain when full daylight broke. Clayton enjoyed how chickens, in particular, would try to fly away right after their heads lay lifeless on the chopping block. They would be flying around, headless, unaware that bodily responses to losing your head were not so instantaneous. Headless bodies hopped up and down with wings beating the air for near to thirty seconds before they would succumb to the inevitable, death. Clayton sighed, wishing people had the same endearing quality as the birds he found mesmerizing.

Alice and Sadie not only had front-row, standing-room-only tickets around the kitchen table for plucking duty, they also were required to take part in the executions. Clayton took great pride in swinging his mighty ax through the necks of helpless birds in front of his eldest girls. He wanted to share with them the thrill and delight of a fresh kill to start the weekend off right. I too probably would have been ushered outside had I been in viewing distance when the decision was made. It was Alice and Sadie's job to hold the chickens' body still on the chopping block while Clayton swung his ax inches from their hands, severing the heads off the terrified birds.

"Go dance with them." Clayton chuckled as he summoned his two traumatized girls to get closer to the chickens that danced around their death ring, unaware that their headless bodies were living out their final spasms until they would collapse, finally allowed the decency to die.

Ray piled the now lifeless bodies onto the counter. The large kettle of water that Beatrice had been simmering had just come to a good rolling boil. Resigned to the fact that this wasn't just another bad dream, I stumbled out of my bed, my nose catching the scent of death that was waiting for me.

As I stood over the metal kitchen table, still in my nightgown, the smell of hot, bloodied feathers cleared my sinuses and helped steam the sleep crystals from my eyes. I knew the routine quite well. Once Beatrice dunked the lifeless bird into the boiling water, it would be my job to pluck every single one of the feathers out of the skin, being careful not to miss any of the pinfeathers in the process. Luckily for me, today's bounty was Rhode Island reds, and their dark-red feathers could be easily seen between the slits of very sleepy eyes.

Beatrice was adept with a razor blade. She could split a hen's belly wide open, dressing it out, guts and all, in just under two minutes. Occasionally, she would cackle with delight coming across a fully developed egg, shell and all, safely tucked inside her warm, naked bird.

I had to work swiftly to keep up with Beatrice. Slow hands were a sign of laziness and wouldn't be tolerated by the devil's wife. As I nimbly worked between half-opened eyes, I wondered if other folks were beginning their Saturday morning the same way we did. Somehow, I doubted it.

Tony and Ray had already loaded up the saws and gas cans while Clayton put his ax away and washed his hands. Work up in the woodlot would be next on the list of chores, and Tony and Ray had gotten used to Saturdays being their day to work while Clayton wandered the woods deep in thought.

While the men worked, the women would finish up the birds and work on the Saturday chores that would take up the rest of the morning and early afternoon. It was always a relief to see what the dinner meat was, up close and firsthand. Beatrice would either boil the chicken or bake it, but either way, there would be no mystery dinner this day.

I had gotten it in my head that if Clayton came home in a good mood, I would talk to him about getting a pet. I knew that Saturdays were the best days to catch Clayton for a few minutes of conversation. Washday and the promise of a night on the town did much for Clayton's spirit and hopefully would put him in a giving mood. I did an extra good job at weeding the designated rows in the field that were assigned to my Saturday chores. I wanted to be agreeable with Beatrice in case I needed her help with my request.

By noon, Clayton's worn-out logging truck pulled into the yard. Ray headed in one direction in search of cold ones as Tony made a beeline for the door that led to his bath before wrestling practice.

I didn't like talking to Clayton and would have much preferred to be seen and not heard, but as Clayton lingered behind to inspect his apple trees, I saw the opportunity. *Now or never.*

Clayton seemed surprised to find me standing behind him. He hadn't summoned me to his side, so he knew I had something up my sleeve in one form or another.

"I want a rabbit, a pet rabbit of my very own," I blurted it out before I lost my nerve.

Clayton started to chuckle and then paused for a moment as he pulled his pouch of chewing tobacco from his back pocket.

"So, you think you want a bunny rabbit, right? Well, if you want to talk to me, you have to ask me like a man."

Clayton pulled out a wad of Redman chewing tobacco and presented it to me. I didn't dare refuse even if Clayton did seem to be in an unusually good mood.

"Put this between your gums and ask me like you really mean it. Don't be a pansy ass about it. Tell me like a man."

Somehow the fact that I was not quite eight years old and a little girl to boot had gotten lost on Clayton. I had come this far, and as long as I didn't throw up on his shoes, I figured it was all a part of beating Clayton at his own game. The size of my chew was just short of a small chicken's egg. It required both of my hands to pack my mouth with the foul stuff.

"I vant a abbit. Pease, let me ave a abbit." I couldn't close my mouth all the way without swallowing the portion of the wad wedged between my tonsils and my palate. I knew I sounded ridiculous, but, by damn, regardless of the burn that was making my chest tingle, my head spin, and my stomach churn, I wasn't backing down.

"Well, why didn't you say so then?" Clayton shrugged as he turned to walk inside. "I like rabbits too, especially when you pair one up with some new potatoes." Clayton couldn't resist laughing at his own joke, his own cruel joke.

What hadn't already slid down my throat had found its way up and out of my mouth with the projectile vomiting that came on instantaneously, splattering my shoes and the rest of me. Tears welled up in my eyes as I stood there alone on the front lawn, wondering if God could just take me now instead of waiting. After a few minutes, I realized that none of my wishes were going to come true and sat down on the front steps waiting for my turn at the gray bathwater.

Chapter 48

WATCHERS

I could feel the wet heat from their breath thick in the air. At first, I stood in utter disbelief at what was happening right before my eyes. Tigers, now tigers? To what end? For what reason? Had I not spent enough nights, too many dreams, outrunning the long, twisted threatening snakes down the forest trails only to lose my footing at the exact moment when I was taking the lead? Had I not bravely stood by wolves in the darkest of nights with my heart wildly beating in my chest? Actually, how ironic it had turned out that the wolves had proven themselves to be a source of unexpected comfort, a form of protection. Powerful wolves had come to sit to my left and to my right, guarding me, protecting a waif, protecting me. Strong and directive, these animals were not pets and could have simply ripped me to shreds in the blink of an eye. Yet somehow, I was in their charge, my safety their responsibility. I was not invisible to the wolves, and how precious that had turned out for someone with nothing to give in return, someone simple like me.

Powerful paws pressed the ground with force enough to cause the exhale of the beast to make a huffing sound rather than an actual breath. The hauntingly beautiful patterns of golden-orange and black swayed back and forth across their rib cages with each of their graceful movements. It was clear that they were making their way to the porch and even clearer that the front two tigers were in charge, leading the march up the back steps.

Holding my breath, I prayed that this was just another dream, another parade, another visitation from Noah's ark. If I could just pinch myself, pinch hard enough, maybe I would simply wake up, or was I already awake?

Dear God, what would I do if nightmares hadn't brought in the tigers but life had?

The house was still, quiet and dark. The tigers roamed methodically from each room to the next. A short trip to where I was hiding now in my bed. I did not hear any movements from my siblings, nor from my parents' room.

Had the other family members left? Had they known of the tigers' arrival in advance? Did they slip out into the night without waking me, without taking me with them?

It felt surreal, in the next moment, realizing that there could actually be something even more terrifying than the monsters, than the boogeyman that I already lived with. As I stared out into the darkness of the tiny bedroom, suddenly the moonlight through the curtains caught the reflection from one of the beasts' eyes, and I found myself looking directly into my most terrifying nightmare of all. Barely inches apart, I gazed into the tiger's eyes, afraid that any movement on my part would have dire consequences. The tiger did not blink, its pupils becoming larger and larger, tiring from its fixed stare.

Maybe I was invisible to the tiger after all? Why had it come within inches, only to stare without seeing me, without destroying me? In disbelief, I watched as the tiger slowly turned around, giving the room to the darkness, once again. Had the tigers' mission been accomplished, or would they return another night, another day? All I knew for certain was that it was time for that pinch, a good, deep pinch to my forearm to bring me up and out of whatever nightmare had found me once again.

Chapter 49

YOU THINK YOU ARE PRETTY?

Winter came, putting a bitter chill in the air. Clayton had never put insulation in the walls or up in the attic, too expensive and a waste of money, so the winter chill could be felt through the curtains, which slightly swayed over the windowpanes while the northern winds blew outside.

When the pair of woodstoves were fired up, causing the stovepipes to glow red hot, the inside of the house was well over a hundred degrees. Beatrice had had the bright idea to tinfoil the entire wall that was directly behind the stove in the living room. She knew that it would help keep the warmth in the room. To me, I felt suffocated, trapped in a bonfire, and wrapped like a Boy Scout foil pack meal, thrown on the coals to cook.

It took all of fifteen minutes for a stick of butter right out of the refrigerator to melt down to liquid while sitting on the kitchen table. Hot was hot, and the woodstoves in our tiny house became indoor infernos.

With no other heat source, building up the fires for the evening meant that by eleven o'clock, the wood was no more than glowing embers that provided little heat or warmth. Beatrice had seen to it that every thrift-store blanket, regardless of color, shape, or size had made it to the back of her station wagon and to each of our beds come winter. After heaving up the blankets in order to crawl underneath them, we felt like we were sleeping underneath a mattress with someone already asleep on the top of it.

Though Clayton was always up by four thirty to fill up the woodstoves, it didn't mean that the house wasn't below freezing temperatures for at least four hours prior. Water left standing in the sink would have a slight crust of ice over it by morning, and any water glass left with a beverage would be rock solid when the temperature shifted inside to freezing cold.

Clayton, psychopath or not, had an amazing creative side. Ordinary words could be spun into the most incredible ditties and stories ever imaginable. According to Clayton, germs played and frolicked all around the house when it was warm inside. Each night, when the temperatures would get below freezing, they would huddle in a corner, trying to maintain warmth from the cluster they created with the others' bodies. By morning, when they saw that the woodstove was roaring with heat and warmth, they would run at top speed to the stove and jump right in through the door. Each germ would meet its demise by burning up in the flames, and the whole process would start over again, each day with another group, a new set of germs.

Along with the bitter chill came snow and ice. But even more treacherous than those combined, Clayton would be home, unable to go to the woods and put in a day's work. Instead, he set aside ample time to fuss with the Lord and drink himself into a stupor all the while the snow outside piled up to the middle of our front door.

Trapped like a snowshoe rabbit caught in a snare, there was little space to hide in, under, or behind. Being in full view of an angry Clayton left us exposed to his nastiness now amplified, which might have otherwise been diffused while he worked hauling logs and falling trees.

Clayton set about tacking up various pictures of women all over the girls' bedroom walls. There were pictures of women ripped out of Beatrice's magazines as well as the cardstock photograph of legs in pantyhose from the newly unwrapped pantyhose that Clayton had found in Alice's dresser drawer. Smiling faces, fancy hairdos, full breasts, fancy dresses, and long legs sporting pantyhose resistant to snags and pulls were plastered as far as the eyes could see.

Clayton wanted to foster an aura of lesbianism, hoping to create excitement by the sheer look of all those women on printable paper.

Unfortunately for Clayton, all of his hard work had been lost on me, as I didn't quite understand what the point of the pictures was and simply figured Clayton was having another one of his crazy spells.

Shortly before bedtime, on the coldest night of the winter thus far, Clayton made the decision that his three girls were not thinking about him as much as we should be. He had overheard talk between us that sounded a lot like vanity to him. In reality, it was probably nothing more than conversation comparing to see who had the hairiest legs. As interaction was strictly monitored and restricted most of the time, it couldn't have actually been about much at all.

Clayton brought us to the kitchen, each of us standing there barefoot, still in our nightgowns. Lining us up against the sink counter, Clayton proceeded next to go into the bathroom, retrieving a sleeve of razor blades.

After returning back to the kitchen, he reached up into the cabinet, reaching to the top shelf where he kept his box of fancy, well-sharpened butcher knives, used only "for special occasions."

"So you sluts think you're fucking pretty, do you?" Clayton spat out, spraying us with a mixture of hard alcohol and tobacco juice. Resting the bulk of his body weight, leaning hard against the kitchen counter, enabled Clayton to use his hands for tasks other than keeping himself upright.

"See these fucking razor blades? Do you know how many ways I could slice up your faces? Wouldn't be so fucking pretty then, would you? Meat hanging down to your ears wouldn't be so hard to picture, now would it? Answer me, little fuckers!" Clayton raised his voice to make us refocus our attention from the sharp little razors being swung inches from our faces up to meet his crazed, dilated blue eyes instead.

"No, sir," we breathed out, only loud enough for him to know that we had responded.

"Maybe we should take off a couple other body parts too, while we're at it. These knives should be sharp enough, don't you think?"

Clayton lightly grazed each of our necks with the longest butcher knife in the box, slowly and methodically, choosing his knives in the order that would instill as much horror as possible.

"Fucking chop each of you tramps up into little bitty pieces and feed you to the pigs. Who wants to go first?"

Beatrice watched the night's entertainment from her favorite front-row seat.

Observing quietly, she busied her hands with the leftover hair in her lap, her favorite chair positioned just right so she could see activity in every corner of the house from her perch. She watched over us like a prison warden overseeing her prison yard. A mixture of amusement and detachment helped to form a twisted, crazed smirk on her face that made her look like an attraction from a low-budget spook house.

She had learned her lesson about getting involved in Clayton's business.

Her ribs still creaked and moaned all on account of opening her mouth the last time. Simple, cautious words had been too threatening to an already enraged Clayton.

"Don't kill 'em, Clay. I don't care if you rough them up, but don't go too far." Even Beatrice could show tenderness when tested. She would wait, watch, and be ready to run if he started cutting this time.

Complete and utter terror has a funny taste all of its own. It leaves a bitter, acidy, tangy flavor that stings the back of your palate, causing your throat to constrict. In great peril, your mind tries to distract you, protecting you from the imminent danger in front of you. Moving beyond the flight-or-fight instincts, your mind begins to disengage as your head becomes heavy and clouded, caught between passing out and being unable to blink.

Your heart starts to gallop fiercely but gets stuck on your chest wall, causing moments of intense pain, feeling as if it is being flung with great force against your rib cage. In that moment, you feel like the tiny sparrow that is trapped behind glass, slamming its body, breaking bones, bewildered as to why it just cannot go through the unrelenting, uncooperative air.

Next comes an even darker round of emotions. Immobilizing, yet with an adrenaline rush much like an engine in park, racing with rpms in the hundreds, feelings are overtaken by rage, I demand the fear to be over, challenging it to be done. Goading my attacker to finish now once and for all with his sick and horrendous deed. Knowing in the end that the screaming that rattles in my brain simply lies silent upon my tongue. Staring up into eyes that should have loved me, I find the final emotion, surrender.

Surrender becomes the internal need to simply give up—the end to the task, the finality of the battle. As a final betrayal, I can see my mother watching intently. If only she had cared, if only she had wanted to.

Unexpectedly, a sudden rush of air fills my lungs as I realize that the knives are now sitting back on the table, razor blades tossed aside.

"Bunch of cocksuckers, get your asses back to bed. Maybe I will just wait and fucking kill you in your sleep instead, you ugly sons of bitches."

Clayton's intoxication was making him feel oozy, and his game was losing his interest. Always time to finish with his threat later.

Somehow the horrors of the night had passed with no bloodshed.

Forming attachments to each other had been dangerous. How could we connect to each other when everything in our life was so badly disconnected? Friendships would have to wait for a safer time, a better time—a time when life wasn't so shattered, a time when it was safer to feel.

Would we reach that day? Was there such a thing?

"Now I lay me down to sleep, I pray the Lord my soul to keep. If I should die before I wake, I pray the Lord my soul to take. Oh, Father, please keep me normal in all of my despair. Amen."

Chapter 50

SANTA CLAUS IS
COMING TO TOWN

Beatrice had been up and down the ladder leading to the attic for the better part of the morning. With a box or two at a time, she struggled to right herself up the ladder without the use of her busy hands.

"Quit watching me and get the hell out of this room!" Beatrice yelled from above my head. Unbeknownst to me, Beatrice was hiding boxes of wrapped presents up in the attic rafters.

Beatrice, with her uncanny ability to detect motion of any kind within a fifty-yard radius, had sensed movement below. Being as careful as I could on tiptoes, I edged my way toward the stack of cardboard crates, hoping to sneak a look inside. Had one of my siblings ended up in the crosshairs of Clayton's foul temper? Had their fate been laid to rest in a cardboard box?

Each of us had experienced a good morning shaking as well as a temperament check shortly before the sun had come up. The night before had been a rough one, complete with a host of new images to dream about for months.

"Yes, sir, I've been shook, but I'll take another."

Like a child's drawing on an Etch A Sketch, the memories of razorblades and knives had been shaken away, no longer showing on the surface, erased temporarily, hidden from view by the untrained eye and stuffed deep into our memories—blades that would continue to cut and harm each of us from within our forgotten selves.

Fortunately, the boxes seemed only to contain crinkled and heavily taped packages, jammed and squashed into their designated cardboard homes.

Shortly after breakfast with the roads clear enough for passage, Clayton left to inspect the damage done by the wintry mix up on the hill. Tony, having been dismissed from duty on account of the weather, had eagerly offered to pick up an extra shift at his mundane fast-food counter job in town—anything to get out of the house when all he really wanted was to sleep and be left alone to stay in his room with his thoughts.

Alice had recently lost her family ranking, as Clayton had moved on to other family members in his quest to destroy and maim equally.

Fortunately, with her diminished role, she was able to persuade Beatrice and Clayton that spending time looking for work in the nearby town would help to keep her from being "underfoot." She would stay with Nanny during the winter break and help her out by doing chores.

Nanny had soft, feathered beds and streetlamps. Alice knew she belonged in that world much more completely than the dank and dismal world she had grown up in. Of course, living "high class," as she had heard many times from a raging Clayton, wasn't the life for a "rag doll" like her.

Alice longed to connect with the real world she knew was out there—a world where impossible dreams came true and people like Beatrice and Clayton didn't exist.

***

Sadie, bundled up in heavy winter clothes, set out to feed and water the hundred or so chickens. A job less than perfect had recently cost her a nasty split lip. Clayton had been convinced that Sadie's mood was lacking the standard enthusiasm required for her task. This blatant show of neglect would not be tolerated under Clayton's regime. He had split her lip, a deep and nasty cut that should have received stitches. Clayton was quite pleased with his handiwork and felt it was a necessary lesson in response to Sadie's insubordination.

Sadie remained out in the coop for the better part of the morning.

With the steady cackle and banter from the animals she so wanted to despise, sitting on the feed bucket, she took solace in time spent alone.

Beatrice's mood fluctuated between teary and moody. Packages now securely in the rafters, she began her rant about Curtis, another replay from yesterday and the day before that. It seemed Curtis would not be coming home for Christmas. School had made him a big-shot, according to her.

Fortunately, however, the fat envelope of cash money that Nanny gave Curtis on each special occasion would soon be delivered. Being firstborn male had always come with privileges and cash dividends. This time, the envelope wouldn't be tucked into the branches of the Christmas tree to be gloated over by an overindulged Curtis. This would be the first of many installment payments collected by an entitled Beatrice for all her extra care and attention.

Curtis was not dead as Clayton had tried to convince us months back. I was relieved to hear Beatrice go on and on about a very much alive Curtis. I was also a little confused too. How had he died and then been expected back for Christmas? Of course, it didn't make sense, but things rarely did.

Curtis was not dead at all. So why on earth would he want to come back here anyway? Although he was treated much better than the rest of us, he still hated the holidays and hated us equally. Any occasion would find Curtis off by himself, deliberately staying away from the rest of us. Even when it was clear that Santa loved him best, he couldn't so much as give a smile or say, "Merry Christmas," or anything even remotely like that to any of us. Holidays were days at the bank for Curtis and not much else.

Christmas meant that Beatrice would be baking up a storm—fruitcake, cookies, chocolate-covered cherries, no bakes, date bars, pumpkin pies, and apple pies among several others. Each one carefully cooled and then popped into a Ziploc and sent to the freezer. Like clockwork, about three days before the twenty-fifth rolled around, she would set out her bounty of sugar all around the house on cheap plastic Santa-faced trays, giving the go-ahead for us to fill up on holiday cheer.

Maybe it was her way of doing penance, her way of trying to wipe the slate clean. Whatever the reason, we each gained significant weight around the holidays and thanked Santa for helping us to forget the rest of the year.

Next would come the endless yards of silver garland Beatrice would tape, drape, or staple up all along the doorways and along the tops of the walls and the edges of each of her many wooden shelves that lined the living room walls. Statues of Mary, Paul, and Jesus were introduced to Hollywood, as their feet now rested on a bed of bright, shiny holiday tinsel and a splattering of twinkling lights.

Woolworths had seen to it that even the poorest brood could honor Christmas by putting their plastic reindeer, Santas, nativity scenes, and the like all on deep clearance each year right after Christmas. Beatrice had managed to hook up with some of those deals, and we had a bounty of every size, shape, and poseable Santa that any culture had ever dreamed up. Santa and his identical kin would peer down at us from every possible corner of the living room area. Luckily for Beatrice's Jesus, his picture had landed back in the only room that didn't look like someone had just vomited up Christmas—Beatrice's bedroom.

Each year, Clayton dragged home the ugliest balsam fir that he could find to serve as our Christmas tree. This year would be no exception. Like everything else mandated from the big book of rules, Christmas trees had requirements. First and foremost, it could not have more than one decent, plausible side. Corners were designed to conceal flaws on three sides of any tree, so according to Clayton's logic, a one-sided tree with sparse branches was "good enough."

Next, the tree could have no more branches than two sets of Christmas lights could rest upon—waste not want not. A dozen or so ancient glass ornaments were carefully added to the few branches as well as a dollar's worth of twelve-inch silver tinsel. At only ten cents a box, Beatrice could drape that shiny stuff onto our tree until it looked just about the same color as the wall directly behind the stovepipe. The glare from the tree bounced off the living room walls, hitting the tinfoil just right, creating a recreation of the North Star right smack-dab in the center of our dirty living room.

Some years, the two strands of lights were set on the tree with the electrical prongs resting up high in the branches with no hope of ever finding an outlet. The lighting of the tree generally didn't last long enough to bother with. The only real reason was just to test the strand of lights for burned-out bulbs.

"Electricity isn't free … Too much a fire hazard to light up a tree indoors," said the man with glowing red chimney pipes always one spark away from a chimney fire.

Christmas trees had a shelf life of about three days. At the stroke of 6:00 a.m. on the morning of December 26, all holiday evidence would be torn down, boxed up, and swept away, no exceptions! Like everything else, Christmas would be erased, removed from our thoughts on demand.

"Yes, sir, I've been shook, but I'll take another."

This year would play out as it always did—same record, same song.

Regardless of how healthy I was the rest of the year, I always spent Christmas Day sick. Whether it was the excitement of Santa or just the cold North Country temperatures bearing down on our small shack, I succumbed to sickness. Double ear infections, tonsillitis, stomach flu, skin infections, and the most recent, a nasty infection with drainage from the rusty nail that I had knelt on while assisting with the tree stand, consisting of two crisscrossed boards. This unfortunate event eventually turned into a major infection that required a doctor's visit, several rounds of antibiotics, crutches for a couple of weeks, and a very unstable home life with a very pissed-off father. Wasting money on children was not something he took lightly.

The other holiday tradition that was all mine and fortunately less painful was my desperate attempt to watch *The Grinch Who Stole Christmas*. This classic, all-time favorite came around each December. It didn't matter that the black-and-white Grinch from the ancient picture tube didn't do the Grinch's green skin any justice. Nor did it make any difference that sometimes the picture was fuzzy and snowy, much like the weather outside our windows. The trickiest part about the thirty-minute show, including commercials, was that it usually fell during Clayton's television time. Watching the "Whos" became a test of wills, coupled with a lot of prayer that Clayton would either go to bed early or disappear into the bathroom for thirty minutes.

Clayton had his own traditions during Christmas, his sinister mind never resting. Getting rip-roaring drunk and beating the shit out of Beatrice were the ones on the top of his holiday to-do list. Usually, he couldn't wait for Christmas Day to enjoy his favorite festivities and would set about using Beatrice as a punching bag on Christmas Eve, just as midnight Mass was replaying for the third time on the television set. Beatings always seemed to relax Clayton, helping him to work out his anxieties, calming him down so he could really enjoy the blessed holiday.

This Christmas Eve had come with a good mix of northern snow flurries.

Beatrice had been staring out the window in the kitchen door, deep in thought, probably reflecting on the beauty of the holiday but likely more on the beating she would be receiving this evening. After a few moments of quiet time, Beatrice turned to the work at hand and began to busy herself with the holiday Pyrex dishes, condiment bowls, and a stack of fine china known as the Santa plastic plates that she was retrieving from the high cupboard shelves. Plenty of dishes to wash once the turkey was prepared.

I had set about chopping cups of celery for the dressing that would stuff the twenty-pound bird thawing in the kitchen sink. Making my way last to the dreaded yellow onions, which soon enough, would burn and sting my eyes, causing them to tear up and run like a water faucet.

"Mom, did Santa bring you presents when you were a little girl?" I questioned, really just thinking out loud.

"No, but he always brought Pa a bottle. You know, Helen, Santa doesn't just go around giving free gifts; he expects something in return." Beatrice turned, waiting for my response.

"Santa has always been really good to us, brings lots of presents and clothes to wear for the whole year. I know he reads my letter every year too."

What was I thinking? Regret lumped up in my throat as the last sentence parted from my youthful lips.

The smile on Beatrice's face was enough to tell me that this kind of bonding time was taking an ugly turn.

"Santa expects you to be good all year long, Helen. Not to ask for anything and to behave yourself and do exactly what your parents tell you to do. Santa expects you to keep your evilness quiet and all to yourself, not telling anyone anything about this family. Remember nothing is for free, no matter who or what you believe in."

Age had set in, leaving me with a flurry of questions just itching to be asked. I had recently stared at the stovepipe long enough to know that no jolly, fat red-suited man could squeeze his way down it. Knowing good and well that I wouldn't like the answers forthcoming from Beatrice, who was all too eager to blindside me, I should have stopped while I wasn't ahead. Yet, accustomed to disappointment, I asked what I had been thinking for a while now, "Is Santa Claus real?" hoping that Beatrice would pretend not to hear and continue on with her pile of holiday dishware.

"Well, now that you asked, no, Helen, he is not real. Don't you think it is about time that you figured out the truth anyway? Make-believe is just that, make-believe, crazy stories told to gullible children is all."

Beatrice was enjoying her little talk, and by the way she looked at the onion tears falling down from my cheeks, she was hoping that the sting was from her words and not from them.

The truth had come to hurt me again. There was nothing magical, no jolly man in a red suit; it had all been a joke, pretend. Maybe guilt and misery did carry a hefty wallet, buying toys wrapped in colorful paper, in trade for our freedom, dignity, and silence.

"He sees you while you're sleeping; he knows when you're awake …"

Between my onion tears, the real tears flowed steadily down my face.

Reality had never been magical, never been safe, just a beast waiting in the darkness. Maybe the Grinch knew best. Strip away all the bribes and see what lay beneath it.

Clayton was our Santa Claus, smelling of yesterday's brandy on his stale breath and wearing last week's blood, still on his hands. Santa didn't come calling in a sleigh with reindeer but out of the fires of hell, carrying a pitchfork instead.

Chapter 51

CARPE DIEM

Seize the day and never look back. Tony would have given anything to have a normal family, to be a part of something created out of love and hope instead of pain and heartbreak. Behind his dark, handsome features and boyish charm was a sensitive young man full of talent and zest, caught in an invisible collar attached to a family chain of violence and pain.

Tony embraced the goodness that seemed to flow to him whenever he was away from his miserable upbringing. The confident Tony became captain of the soccer team and of the wrestling team and could run track faster than any of his teammates. Tony's topnotch speed made him seem like he was running for his life out on the track. In a way, that was exactly what he did.

Strong, eager, and attractive, Tony was a high school athlete, popular with his friends, as well as the ladies.

Tony liked to sing, even though he wasn't fond of singing in front of others. Music spoke from within, telling a story much too personal to sing out loud and be heard. Gifted with the ability to write, Tony created an amazing school play production that he performed for his entire class as well as the underclassmen. Yes, the confident Tony soared, high above the ugliness, high above the horrors that haunted him, memories of drawn shades and sisters' screams.

He was voted class clown by his graduating class; his peers loved him. They laughed with him and would have never imagined that the Tony they knew carried deep scars of abuse, both physical and mental. "Big Tony" was the name that resonated throughout the gymnasium each and every time this 145-pound wonder stepped out onto a wrestling mat. Tony was the best, and by damn, he had to be. In seventeen seconds, he could take down a man under a count of three, either in his weight class or higher, and then jump to his feet and wave hello to the folks in the bleachers, standing tall with his glistening, sweaty wavy black hair, his incredible winner's smile, and a touch of arrogance that suited him well.

Big Tony was a winner. The crowds told him so by their chants and through their methodic stomping on the bleachers. No one really knew why it meant so much to Tony to win, why losing wasn't an option at all. No one would have believed that the disheveled man in the bleachers who sat watchful and patient was determining Tony's fate once the bell rang and the bleachers cleared for another night. Clayton didn't accept losers into his house.

Clayton came to most matches, as a part of him wanted Tony to screw up so he could retaliate against him, make him stay outside as punishment for not proving his worth. Losing was dangerous and would cost Tony more than a match.

At school, Tony could take charge of his own life. He could make decisions that he felt good about. No one knew the other side of his life. He could never trust anyone with his secrets, as people wouldn't understand, would judge him harshly for the sins of his father and his mother.

The Tony who lived in Clayton's house was also restless, anxious, and often angry. Tony referred to Clayton as the "old man" when Clayton wasn't in hearing distance. Tony hated the fear that would linger, taking away his courage, taking away his confidence. Tony began sneaking out of his bedroom window late at night and started hanging out with a crowd that enjoyed a good party. Marijuana and hard alcohol usually were the starters of the party, followed by whatever the bad guys could beg, borrow, or steal from around town. LSD was a happening drug of the era, and it seemed to help take the edge off the images of horror that liked to dance around Tony's head when the pot began to wear off.

The battle between the confident Tony and the beaten-down Tony began to rage within him. After a late-night rendezvous with the local guys, Tony came home to a power-hungry, crazed Clayton who had discovered his son missing from his room hours before. Clayton had waited, alert and anxious for the beating he would administer to his disobedient yellow canary son.

The loud, abusive fight pierced the night like a train wreck. If it hadn't been for the solitude that lay a mile or so on each side of the property line, neighbors would have assuredly called out the authorities to see what the racket was all about.

Clayton shoved Tony against the door, bouncing the back of his head hard on the door casing with the force of the impact. "Get to fuck out and don't ever fucking come back!"

With just a moment to reach for his jacket and a handful of personal items, Tony was ejected from the house—a free man yet without a single place to go. The next day, Beatrice drove to the police station and filled out a report that stated without question that her youngest son was to be officially declared an emancipated minor. She was not going to take any responsibility for anything that might happen to him from that point forward.

She had felt uncomfortable about Clayton kicking out her minor son, but she had to live with Clayton and didn't want any more trouble for herself either.

Tony had a lot of decisions to make, a lot of loose ends to tie up. Sleeping under the stars at the local reservation state park would work for a while, but it wouldn't be everything. Tony was too smart to stay down for long. He hadn't really known what to do when he had gotten his letter in the mail.

Unlike Curtis before him, Tony had been watching the mail, had been waiting for any news of the future.

"Ready or not, here I come." Tony's thoughts spoke loudly in the darkness. Kicking the sand off the back of his legs, while rereading the letter deeply creased from indecision, Tony made his mind up. He was going to use that full scholarship he had been awarded. Tony was going to be big man on campus at Potsdam State College.

Chapter 52

PRISON-STRIPED TWIN

With the boys gone and Alice spending every free moment away at Nanny's house, Sadie and I were getting moved out of our current sleeping arrangement. It wasn't so much that Clayton cared whether or not we were comfortable or gave any thought about the additional leg room we would be receiving but mostly that Beatrice wanted to expand their bedroom by knocking out the wall between the two rooms. After all those years of sleeping behind a curtain rod, Sadie and I were going to share a bedroom complete with a door, door hinges, and a doorknob. Privacy had been a luxury only afforded to the boys. Sadie and I were keeping our fingers crossed that Clayton wouldn't start connecting the dots and come calling with a screwdriver to renovate the boys' old bedroom.

The grouchy woman in the curtain had been paying fewer visits over the last several months. I wondered how she would take the news that we were no longer behind the curtains that she used as a makeshift shawl for her impromptu visits. Unfortunately, I was still the only one who ever saw her floating at the bottom of the curtain, so for the sake of not being ridiculed, I continued to keep it to myself. I wondered if she could float through wood or maybe she would start keeping a watchful eye on Beatrice and Clayton now that we were less convenient.

Sadie and I were spending far fewer nights in the car, as I had learned to tame my nightmares and squelch the screams that had been a major part of my life thus far. With maturity came the ability to scream in silence and to wake up instead of waking everyone else up. Unfortunately, with maturity, I still hadn't been released from my shameful, awful embarrassment of bedwetting. Maybe the newness, the novelty of better sleeping quarters would help me to control my inability to stay dry. I was hopeful and would make an extra effort to include this request in my prayers at night.

The old dresser had anchored me high enough that in stormy, wet weather, the narrowness of the hull had kept me dry as it flowed downstream throughout the dresser drawers to the floor, allowing quick and easy access with all evidence being wiped up with an old dirty rag from under the sink.

I was horribly embarrassed and terrified of the verbal and physical assault that would come my way each and every time Beatrice noticed the yellow stains on my sheet. Fortunately for me, the old wringer washer didn't see sheets on a regular basis. No matter how many nights I spent awake, quietly shaking my wet sheet or blowing on it to dry it into a dull stain, I could never catch myself before the deed had already been done. The coldness and wetness during the harsh winter months were added to my list of embarrassing things I would have to forgive myself for later when I was older and less afraid.

With fewer mouths to feed and a steady stream of income coming in from the still lucrative business of having a woodcutter for a husband, Beatrice started spending her time and money in making the house "a little nicer."

Beatrice could stretch a single dollar so it would reach around the moon and back if she had to. Interior design had become a new interest of hers, and she set about stripping wallpaper and buying metal paintbrushes on deep winter clearance. Wallpaper paste quickly became her newest fascination. She seemed to make it by the gallon buckets. Suspiciously it looked like the foul-tasting oatmeal that we shoveled down on cold mornings as well as fed to the dogs that Clayton had agreed to keeping as long as they "stayed outside and away from us."

Beatrice's obsession with changing the scenery evolved into a frenzy of sewing colored bedsheets into new curtains, painting all walls not already plastered in wallpaper, and changing the entire look of each room almost every season. Night after night, the ugly drama continued to play out with the same tired cast members but surrounded by Beatrice's latest and greatest new, colorful set.

As her ambitions grew, Beatrice wore the crown of rummage-sale queen. Boasting that she could find a bargain where normal people would never even think of searching. Her next mission was to find a mattress for me to replace the worn-out mattress on the bottom bunk that had clearly seen better days. Tattered and already used even before Tony had slept on it, it had begun to release its stuffing all over the "new" carpet that Beatrice had found out at the corner of some rich person's house in town.

"People always throw the damndest things away."

Loading Sadie and me up for our free car ride, carrying the latest classified ads, Beatrice set out to purchase a used mattress with the five-dollar bill she had taken from Clayton's wallet. If she had to travel to Canada for a bargain, she had enough gas in the car to do it.

I hated the thought of sleeping on another person's mattress. As if my very turbulent world wasn't already bad enough, I had begun to figure out that I too was different. I could see people that my sister could not see; I could close my eyes and visit different rooms, different places, and, hell, different countries. I was not like them, not like anybody that I knew. I hated to wear the hand-me-downs, hated to wear the nickel britches from the thrift store. I could feel each of the owner's personalities, could feel them, could see them, and hated not knowing why. I couldn't wear somebody else's clothes without carrying on a dialogue with the person later. I felt all of them, knew them, and was terrified that they knew me as well.

It goes without saying that used mattresses come from very strange places. Rich people throw them out with their trash, and poor people sell them for pennies on the dollar. After visiting a multitude of poor families with probably similar situations, Beatrice found an old twin prison mattress with almost an entirely good side left to it. It seemed like the whole world came with stains and spills, and this mattress looked like it had been flipped a couple of times in its lifetime. It smelled of tobacco, filth, and cold dirt. As luck went, it was now officially mine. My new bed companion fit nicely on the roof of the old station wagon tied down. I hoped the drive home would help to beat the smell out of it before I had to be introduced that night to its previous owner.

Beatrice was ecstatic with her purchase. With the leftover change, she was able to buy a sizeable amount of plastic flowers at a rummage sale on the way home. In a good mood, Beatrice serenaded us all the way back to the States, singing her version of an old Loretta Lynn favorite, "Like a Bird."

"Now I lay me down to sleep, I pray the Lord my soul to keep. Oh, God, just keep me normal. Jacques doesn't like me sleeping on his bed. He smells of women and tobacco. I'm so tired; I have to go to sleep. Heaven help me, please!"

Chapter 53

RAISE THE CANDLES HIGH

So raise the candles high
'Cause if you don't, we could stay black against the night …
—Melanie Safka, "Lay Down"

Life had always been a fight. You were at war with those who were supposed to be on your side as confidantes, as allies. What the hell was wrong with the world when a child's greatest enemy slept soundly in the room next door?

Smart, crafty, and with a thirst for better, Alice dug her heels in and refused to be damaged, refused to live in travesty. Rise above, claw your way out if need be. Look straight ahead, and if the next step so happened to land on the backs of those in the trenches with you, then so be it. Life was a game, and not everyone was going to end up a winner.

Anger can be an amazing catalyst, propelling you forward, pushing through the emotional waste that tangles up under your feet, tripping you into believing that the grass is *not* greener on the other side. Alice knew it was; it just simply had to be. Nanny, though not interested in providing the emotional support of a grandmother, did provide refuge, a safe haven for Alice to dream, to grow stronger. The big day would soon arrive. It was almost time. In hindsight, Alice knew that in the end, it could all be summed up into a few powerful words, leaving the rest behind, "No big deal."

The future was not about remembering; it was about forgetting, cutting losses, severing ties.

A raging bull doesn't simply lower its head for a drink of water but stomps its feet, sending a clear message that it is not to be reckoned with before it looks away from potential danger. Alice hadn't started out as a raging bull; she simply would have shared if there had been a choice.

Beatrice had tried to groom her into the perfect little victim. She had never suspected that Alice was a lot smarter than that and would eventually turn the tables around, sharing the immense pain in return for elevated status with Clayton. Alice hated the games, but she hated being a victim even more. Her focus had to remain on the prize, the finale, and the moment that she could decide if she ever wanted to look back, it would be her decision and no one else's.

Alice would miss Tony, but he had already made the leap. She would be next. Being so close in age, they had bonded, had shared life outside the bondage of family secrets. Tony would be fine, and so would she. The future would be for reconnecting. Alice would worry about that later; for the time being, other pressing tasks had to take priority, had to come first. Sadie had been not so much a sounding board as a punching bag to an older sister who didn't know how to contain her rage, her fury.

Sadie would continue on with or without her. In time, she might forget too.

Sentiment would be buried, put aside like an old toy. Life was calling her name, and like a flight leaving the town Misery, she didn't want to be late for it.

Packing had been an easy task. Nice things cost a lot of money. A few nice things were better than a lot of regular stuff. Alice's possessions fit nicely in an overnight bag that she had found at a specialty store in town.

With her dignity in tow, a copy of *Elle* under her arm, her newly blond hair blowing in the wind, Alice and her eating disorder boarded the plane, heading to anywhere far away, never to be seen by her family again.

Another one of my siblings had been officially declared dead by Clayton.

Part 4

OUTSIDERS

Hope is a difficult concept to sustain.

Chapter 54

VISITORS

"Bitches need to keep that goddamn door open." Clayton's foul mood could be heard from the living room where he was busy stoking the woodstoves with the last of the winter wood that had been stacked against the tinfoil wall.

Some black ground beetles, startled awake from their long winter resting spot, no longer protected by wood and darkness, scurried across the dirty living room carpet, blending in with the ground in dirt and stains from many seasons passed. Winter had been a long and tedious event and still threatened a good night's worth of frost.

Though I missed my siblings, I remained encouraged knowing that each had managed to safely escape, following each other's lead like dominoes. In return for the increasing solitude and loneliness, I had to admit I was forming an attachment to their abandoned sleeping quarters. Feeling a bit safer than I had felt in quite some time, I lay snug between the top bunk and the floor. My bed served a dual purpose—on top, beneath the covers or depending on the emotional, climatic feel of the house, beneath its bottom braces, resting just high enough off from the carpet to scoot under and out of arm's reach.

The stains remained on my twin mattress; fortunately, however, its previous owner had become bored and left, taking the remnants of women and smokes with him. I managed to put a few of Beatrice's blankets underneath my sheet, and the scent remaining had become my own, for better or worse.

The woman in the curtain apparently did not want to come visit now that there was a wooden door between us. I wondered if she had looked around from her post and discovered that what was happening in Clayton and Beatrice's now expanded bedroom gave her nightmares too. Unfortunately, it didn't take long to realize that she wasn't the only spirit that had a connection to our very turbulent world.

This morning's visitor came while Sadie slept soundly on the top bunk. I had just returned from another powerful dream, my heart still racing, my forehead bathed in sweat. Shadows, dark and menacing, had chased me through the woods. As I ran under limited moonlight, I lost my footing on the mounds of jagged rocks and tree stumps. The shadows, aware of my latest predicament, changed form, becoming long, dark slithering snakes, snakes that weaved between my legs, moving upward and hugging the flesh of my inner thighs as their silvery tongues began to vibrate in unison until the deafening sound of their hissing alerted my consciousness to grab at the reins quickly taking me back to my twin mattress, back to temporary safety.

Oh, how I envied the naive girls at school. Their dreams were surely of picnics and puppies, while my slumber lay bruised and infested with unimaginable fear and immeasurable sorrow. My world showed no comparison, no compassion. Our lives ran in different directions, infinite worlds apart.

Clayton's current tirade from the other room distracted me, bringing me back to the misery that was real and festering just a wall away. Closed doors spelled independence, something Clayton would never afford to the lowly, weaker sex, worthless females who lived under his roof. Before long, the door would become nothing more than a decoration, just a constant reminder that freedom and privacy would always be just out of reach. Pretending to be asleep, I hoped that the inevitable drama would be patient and wait for later in the morning to detonate in Sadie's and my face.

At first, the sounds of heavy boots on thinning carpet made me suspect Clayton had sneaked into the room, deciding how best he could terrorize us as his good morning surprise. Threats of bouncing our heads off the floor usually got our attention, especially Sadie's, as she had a much longer drop than I.

Once the heavy boots were silenced, I began to feel a distinctive shaking, a vibration beginning at just the spot my feet, wrapped in heavy winter woolen blankets, rested on the mattress. Subtle at first with no more than a quick nudge, the shaking intensified until the entire bunk rumbled in a quake of motion.

Surprisingly up top, Sadie's breathing had not change its rhythm. Perhaps her mind was choosing to accept the unexpected rocking as an impromptu lullaby. Maybe her subconscious felt it best to protect her, cut her off from the surreal mix of reality just beneath her.

Cautiously, I opened my eyes. Instinctively creasing a smile on my lips in the event I would find myself looking up and into the eyes of a very crafty Clayton. Clayton didn't accept rational responses to circumstances, and sad, fearful faces would only help to ignite his always-a-match-away temper.

Though it was only about five in the morning, the light from the kitchen was painting a splash of bright-yellow, making visibility all around the room quite clear through the now open door. Turning my head slowly, I took in the entire room in full panoramic view. The room was empty, unchanged from the night. A formidable coolness lingered in the air in spite of the climbing temperatures from both woodstoves hard at work.

Had the shaking been my imagination? Had the heavy boots come from the forest? Had the snakes followed me back too? Trying to make sense of it all, once more, I heard the loud clatter of boots taking another half a dozen steps and trailing off toward the wall, the coolness of the room going with them.

This time, my eyes were wide open, staring at the noisy nothingness.

When you live in a house of horror, you never let your guard down.

Always alert and in fight-or-flight mode, your primary struggle is to outsmart, outwit, outlive, and at all cost endure more than any evilness can dish out. Survival can be a daunting task and truthfully, coming out "normal," a constant uncertainty regardless of the mountain of prayers.

Perhaps in the end, normal is simply a place marked, staked by a flag high atop Mount Everest, hidden by the clouds. A continuous climb on a dangerous, rugged, and jagged trail where payment to travel, of passage, becomes pieces of oneself, left behind to bleed out on the rocks. I vowed again, mouthing the words for confirmation that, yes, I would continue the climb, moving forward, fully knowing that if I stopped to look back, I would surely lose my grip and fall to my death. What nagged my thoughts, giving me constant worry, was what if I reached the spot called normal but found it just beyond the other sign marked "trail closed"? Would the detour sign then be pointing straight down?

Clearing my mind and returning back to the task at hand, I wondered if Tony and Curtis had been witnesses to the unworldly visits too? Had they heard the boots, felt their bed shaking? What about the light shows that greeted me, dancing on these walls in the darkness? A ball of light the size of a cantaloupe trailed the length of the wall that ran adjacent to my headboard, making its way across the wall until it disappeared through sheetrock just beyond the foot of my bottom bunk. It was an intense and brilliant white light that seemed to glow from within its center. Sometimes the light would remain for a few moments, lingering on the wall nearest to my head; other times, it would move so fast that my eyes would be unsure of whether or not it had actually been there at all. Had my brothers seen lights too?

Whatever the meaning of the light, whether friend or foe, I only hoped that as I buried my head underneath the mound of heavy covers, the next time I came up for air, the light would be gone.

Chapter 55

SEASON OF THE BEES

April had come, bringing with it tremendous change and plenty of rain showers. Although Clayton's roof over our heads kept us dry, it would never keep us safe. Experience had been a good teacher. Flesh and blood were no reasons and certainly no excuses to go soft, according to Clayton's logic. We remained objects of his desire as well as objects of his rage.

Little did I know that warmer weather would leave me with yet another set of painful scars forever etched into my memory, requiring another metaphorical swipe out of the jar of healing salve, hoping that someday I would still recognize the face that would stare back at me from the mirror.

As the winds continued to blow, I would remember this as the season of the bees.

Winter's chill had been dutifully warmed out of the air by the sun.

Clayton, who was enjoying a lazy day at home, was outside studying one particular honeybee hive from a good distance away. The other hives seemed active as the bees were out looking for flowers and food. However, the hive that caught his attention didn't seem to have any activity whatsoever. Deciding that the bees must be dead or gone, Clayton instructed Ray to bring the hive into the house so Beatrice could rescue the remaining honey before it turned rancid. Ray dutifully carried the heavy box and placed it on top of the old metal kitchen table. The temperature of the house was easily twenty degrees warmer than outdoors. Figuring that it was truly springtime, the lazy, sleepy bees, originally hidden, began to swarm in every room of the house by the thousands, all within seconds. Hibernation was now officially over.

"Get all of those goddamn bees back into the box before I get home. I am allergic to the motherfuckers." Clayton's words trailed off, as he wasted no time backing the old pickup out onto the tarmac.

I would take a beating later for my decision, but ironically, fear had helped me to find the courage to barricade myself in my bedroom with my forbidden door and a handful of kitchen towels blocking the crawl space between the door's edges and the carpet. Beatrice and Ray would have to contend with the stinging demons on their own, beating or not.

As luck would have it, when Clayton returned several hours later, the only evidence remaining of the active bees were specks of yellow bee excrement on every curtain, wall, nook, cranny, and countertop. Fortunately, Clayton hadn't made Ray count the bees prior to their dislodgment; otherwise, he would have known how adept Beatrice had been with the metal fly swatter and how much lighter the hive was now after her handiwork.

Right around the time that the belt marks finally began to fade, Clayton decided that I was old enough to go walking with him in the woods, just the two of us. Clayton wasn't much for the warm, fuzzy stuff so this alone time sounded rather suspicious. Regardless of his failing knees, Clayton could turn on a dime when brush was underfoot and when he was trying to throw off a tail. A man shouldn't be able to run like a gazelle in thorns and thicket, but Clayton did.

It occurred to me about forty-five minutes off from the familiar path, while deep into the woods, the only real purpose for our time together was to see how long it would be before I became completely lost and alone. With Sadie only a handful of years away from making her big escape too, perhaps Clayton figured it was time to remind his youngest who was actually in charge here. Not wanting to become a live meal for Clayton's woodland creatures, I was damn sure to keep up. I wouldn't let him win, not out there.

At full speed, I managed to close the gap to about fifty yards apart.

Clayton, pretending to be deep in thought, ignored my pleas and cries for him to slow down and seemed to have entirely forgotten that I was with him at all. After crossing some fallen trees that ran alongside a small brook, I began to feel an intense burning sensation on the back of my legs. The pain, feeling like a branding iron on my skin, found its way to my back, stomach, arms, and chest. With my fear reaching yet another new level, I started screaming, realizing that Clayton had stirred up a nasty hive of yellow jackets, making them quite agitated and prime for my young skin. As I screamed out in pain, I saw Clayton a safe distance away watching me with his cold eyes and an awful smirk on his face. I began to run toward him, hoping that he would come to his senses and help me. As I approached him, to my horror, he turned and began to walk quickly away.

"Stay the hell away from me," I could hear Clayton's voice from over the hill.

My legs refused to continue as I stopped and stood alone, my throat parched from screaming, my lungs burned from exertion. The enormous surge of adrenaline mixed with the bee venom made my head throb, sending an intense, stabbing sensation throughout my entire body. It was time, time to make peace with myself. If this was the way I would die, I wouldn't go afraid. Normal would have to meet me right here in the forest and simply take me to heaven quietly and without any fanfare. I was ready this time; I had suffered more than enough.

For whatever reason, the stinging stopped. As I opened my eyes, coming to terms with the fact that I was still very much alive, I realized that the yellow jackets had left. No more stinging, no more sound of angry bees. Perhaps I had taken them too far from their home and they were settled with me. As my legs gave out and I landed on the ground, I was able to see the welts that had already begun to take form on my torso, legs, and arms. Hundreds of welts made my skin sweaty and hot to the touch. My stomach, fortunately empty, began to heave up whatever remained after a long afternoon without lunch. I wasn't getting to throw in the towel just yet. I guessed I still had more suffering to do.

Clayton, after seeing that the bees were gone, found his way over to where I had landed in the grass.

"Bet'cha not afraid of bees, now," Clayton said in his sinister way.

Had Beatrice told him that I had hidden from the bees in the house? I would never know. Quite frankly, I didn't care either. All I knew was that I was still alive and Clayton's sick kind of fun had played out and hopefully was done for the day. Keeping a close eye on him as we looped back around to where we started, I couldn't help but notice that his pace had slowed as if the wind had been knocked out of his sails. His prank had given him a good jolt and an adrenaline release, but now it was over and he would have to settle back into just a regular foul mood for a dismal Clayton.

As the engine came to life in the nearly rusted-out Ford, I felt a sudden rush of relief as I closed my eyes, knowing our bonding time was finally over for another day.

Chapter 56

SHACKLED

On the surface, Clayton had taken the news quite well that Beatrice's aging father needed taking care of. Since her mother had died, Pepe hadn't been able to take care of himself without the attention of a woman around to fix him supper, do his wash, and service any of his other needs.

The biggest problem that no one batted an eye over was that Pepe was a full-fledged, fall-down drunk, and anyone with half a lick of sense knew to shut the doors and draw the shades whenever the bastard came crawling for a handout. But being the good people that Beatrice and Clayton pretended to be, they naturally took Pepe in. It went without saying that Pepe became Sadie's and my newest responsibility in an already full day of chores. Clayton was getting a new drinking partner and someone else to play his nasty tricks on, and Beatrice would be getting another opportunity to wipe the slate clean for Jesus.

With all the latest excitement, Clayton got it in his head that he needed a distraction, a diversion of some sort. The latest fun of our bee adventure had worn off and didn't bring a chuckle anymore when Clayton found himself reminiscing over his purposeful pranks. Change was moving into his spare bedroom, and whether he liked it or not, another man would soon be sleeping in his castle. Without any explanation, Clayton, after his regular Saturday walk through the woods, pulled into the yard, toting a large dog that he had tethered by an old rope to the bed of his pickup truck. Clayton had found his diversion.

Rica was a junkyard dog with a nasty disposition. A crossbreed of German shepherd and mongrel, Rica wasn't much of a family dog and we weren't much of a family in return. I never knew quite how he ended up tethered to the back of Clayton's truck, but here he was, now tied to a ten-foot length of thick chain connected to an equally large choker chain collar.

The first couple of days being tethered to a large hardwood tree, Rica managed to go around and around that tree until the last possible turn left his snout wedged up at an angle, lying flush with the bark of the tree.

"Let him choke to death if he is too damn dumb to unwrap himself," Clayton ordered, becoming bored with the whole matter and going inside.

Walking backward, close enough to Rica, I soon discovered that Rica and his wrapped chain would follow my moves, reversing his situation from choking to death to being free again on his stretch of ten-foot chain. I also learned that until he got to know me, I had best be at least eleven feet away when he finally managed to free himself from his predicament. Rica didn't like being on a chain. Behaving like a poor wild stray, he had just been at the wrong place at the wrong time. I wanted to unhook that latch that connected to his collar, chains that made him ours, and let him run far, far away from this awful place. However, I knew his freedom would carry a very high price tag not only for me but also for dumb dogs that might not run fast enough and far enough away. At the prospect of getting beaten and probably bitten all in return for doing the right thing, my trembling hands couldn't find the guts to unsnap the hook.

With bent and twisted ears, Rica was a rough looker. The healed scars that remained hairless all over his head and torso showed that he was no stranger to a fight. He had clearly seen his share of dogfights and probably more than his fair share of human abuse as well. How had this poor creature come across Clayton? Maybe abuse had become too familiar to Rica?

Maybe he had recognized it, possibly even sought it out, or stood frozen against an instinctual response to run? Whatever the circumstances, I knew that Clayton was going to make Rica "take it like a man."

Included in Clayton's big book of rules were instructions on how to properly take care of pets and pet ownership. It wasn't an extensive list but mostly came down to feed it if you remember and let it starve if you don't, followed by, "Leave the son of a bitch alone or he will take off your goddamn hand."

In time, Rica began to understand that you don't bite the hand that feeds you, lest of course it lingers too long at your feeding dish after it has completed its business of laying mush and scraps. Meals, however meager, were still worth fighting for.

As the newness of his surroundings began to fade, Rica went about the business of entertaining himself on his ten-feet of freedom. Running in a half circle to the full extension of his chain became a game of boredom that went on and on unless he was eating or sleeping in his makeshift wooden doghouse. At first, I was grateful that Rica had found a way to occupy his solitude, to find peace with his latest circumstances. As I watched his chain sway back and forth like a pendulum, I became aware that something looked different where choker collar met chain.

The dirty silver collar that had once held a slight dangle below the neckline was all but gone. The rabies tag, begrudgingly bought and paid for "just in case Rica got loose and bit someone," could no longer be seen punctuating his neckline. It was apparent that Rica remained chained but the links of collar were gone, somewhere. With my natural, innate fear of dogs, especially mean ones, I tried really hard to mask my fear behind long, slow breaths. As I reached for the base of Rica's collar, the horror of my discovery made my heart race and my legs begin to shake.

The thick silver chain was buried deep into Rica's neck. The festering, infected flesh that wove itself in and out of the metal links showed that poor Rica's body had done its best to expunge its enemy of metal and steel. The hair that had once provided protection between the nape of the neck and the thickness of the noose of Rica's collar had somehow been turned inside out, knitted between flesh and bone and red, inflamed skin. Not knowing what to do or whom to trust, I ran inside and into Beatrice, who had been watching me all the while from the bedroom window.

"I'm not taking that animal to the vet. Wasted enough money on food for it already. Grab the gallon jug of bleach and disinfect it before it rots off his neck." Beatrice stared down at me, annoyed that I cared so much.

I wasn't a hero, not even close. I would have rather crawled under my bunk and squeezed my eyes tight until the tragedy washed over. Wishing Sadie was there and not off being terrorized by Clayton, I made the only choice I had. Regardless of the warm, oozy, tingly feeling that crawled up and down my back, I had to help. I would never be like Beatrice, cold and uncaring. I would always care even if it hurt. With trembling hands, I set back out the front door with a half a jug of bleach and tears streaming down my face.

I don't know why Rica didn't bite my hand or take my head off with his powerful jaws as I leaned in, untangling metal from flesh. Maybe, Mr. Heavy Boots with his invisible hands had held Rica's head to the side, shielding me from nervous canine teeth. All I knew was by the time I had freed Rica from the sting of the collar, bleached his neck down, and stuck a half of a dishrag between the rungs of the choker and his peeled-back flesh, my clothes were soaked thoroughly and I could barely speak from all of the fear and emotion.

Somehow, Rica's neck didn't rot off. The bleach had boiled out small chunks of dead flesh that probably needed coming out after all the trauma anyway. Rica didn't like anyone touching him for quite a while after his makeshift surgery and instinctively held off on his ritual of half-circle running until the tugging didn't cause any further pain. For me, I felt like we had both gone through something terrible but was thankful that as I watched Rica from the safe side of his territorial half ring, he didn't seem to hold grudges. Little did either of us realize at the time, this wouldn't be the last time that poor Rica felt the sting of bleach running down his neck.

Rica was in store for a lot more suffering; we just weren't there yet.

Clayton had returned back home with Sadie, back from their monthly car ride, which consisted primarily of running over at least two stray dogs on the back roads, more on a good day, and then celebrating his successes with a large soft-serve ice cream cone on the trip back home. Clayton felt that Sadie needed some toughening up and wanted to teach her that only pansies and canaries cry over death. Afternoon hunting trips always seem to calm Clayton down, relieving the built-up tension in his neck and shoulders. As Beatrice filled him in on what trouble I had created with "that damn dog," Clayton seemed amused rather than angry with me. Escaping a potential beating, I could feel my blood finally making its way back down from my scalp to my extremities.

"You dumb ass, that mutt should have taken off your hand for sticking your nose where it didn't belong."

Clayton soon lost interest, deciding what was done was done. After all, he had other things on his mind that needed to be discussed with Beatrice.

I helped Beatrice pop the jig on yet another pressure cooker of boiled supper and carefully placed cabbage, green beans, and ground meat on a plate for Clayton, making sure that tonight's bounty didn't accidentally slide into each other on the plastic supper plate. Meals eaten together were still required—not for the purpose of companionship but so Clayton could inspect each of our plates for any remaining food we thought we were too good for. Fortunately, the old black-and-white television had won out over the rickety kitchen table from previous years. Meals were now served while heavyweight wrestling played as a backdrop, complete with an abundance of narration from an overstimulated and overly opinionated Clayton.

As the dishes began to make their way to the kitchen to be washed and in between elbow drops and scissor kicks blasting from the old black-and-white, Beatrice and Clayton began a serious discussion about money.

Clayton wanted to make sure that Beatrice knew without any doubt that the johns no longer held an interest in her now that she had turned into a "fat ass" and had let herself go. Furthermore, the aging process had not been kind to her, as her tits had begun to sag around near her belly button.

Letting herself go caused a deficit in what she should have been bringing in.

It was time to take the leap, time to make a man's decision about the household finances.

Clayton knew that in just a few days, Pepe would be coming to live with them. Pepe wouldn't be required to pay room and board, though it had crossed Clayton's mind a few times. Family was family, and he would expect his own kids to take him in when he got old and stayed drunk like Pepe. After all, it was time to prove to the rest of the sons of bitches that Clayton didn't throw goddamn family out on the street. Might even take a little fun out of the situation for him anyway. Time to see how much torture an old drunk could hold before he tried to fight back.

Clayton continued on, revealing his answer to bringing some real money into his house. Deciding that his worthless daughters couldn't keep the weeds down anyway on the plot of land just on the other side of the cattails nestled in the family swamp south of the house, he decided that it made one hell of a good spot to open a storefront. He was going to have his own stop and go grocery store complete with a couple of gas pumps out front.

"I'll be king of the corner. All the white trash can come spend their welfare checks at my store. There will be plenty of beer, gas, sub sandwiches, and cigarettes to sell. The cash money will just start flowing right to my door." Clayton's words were mighty powerful, especially to him.

Change was sweeping across the Clayton household like a tornado. First Rica, then Pepe, and now we were going to open up a grocery store. How was Clayton ever going to let us out of the house long enough to wait on his customers? I could feel a powerful storm making its way across the living room—yes, a very powerful one, indeed.

Chapter 57

THAT GIRL AND THOSE GIRLS

Pepe was a mean drunk packaged in a large, hulking build of a man. His bald head was enormous with an unnatural shininess to it. Sadie and I were convinced that his brain, trapped inside the gigantic bowling ball resting on top of his shoulders, was no longer pink but pickled in the endless gallons of beer and grain that had blanched it night after night. Void of any outside entertainment, Pepe became our single source of amusement whenever he was left sitting alone for any length of time without a mind-altering beverage to bring to his lips.

The show always started the same way, slow at first with just a few twitches, a sleight of hand, a jerk to his shoulder. Next, with his large brick-laying, mail-carrying hands, he would chop at the air until just at the right moment when those large hands would land in an ipsilateral manner, falling on both sides of his bald head. The muttering, subtle at first, started as just a whisper under his breath. As his agitation grew and began to take on a life of its own, a string of French Canadian words started pouring out of him.

With the authority of a colonel in the French army and with each foreign syllable, Pepe's hands vigorously rubbed his bald head in time to the beat.

Imagining bees coming from those massive ears, all in a buzz, I knew that Pepe's performance would have earned top spot in the special colored pages of the Sunday funnies. If only he hadn't been so downright awful in spite of his hilarious performance. This was the man who had dragged my grandmother across wooden floors night after night, probably up to the day the cancer took her off to her final resting place. Maybe her intolerance toward grandkids was on account of all her patience being used up forgiving Pepe for his nightly assault on her.

Somehow, it was easy to forgive her. Seeing someone only from the opposite side of a pane of glass that served as the front door to her porch didn't lend itself to much bonding. Sticky fingers no longer had business in her house; her arms didn't ache for the touch of grandchildren. She kept her distance, and in return, we kept ours. Even now, she was probably up in heaven giving the angels the cold-shoulder too.

Pepe never knew our names and became comfortable referring to us individually or as a group as "that girl or those girls." It didn't really bother us that we were nobodies to him. It made ignoring him easier and the disgust we felt inside much more justified, especially on the numerous occasions when he would tuck in for the day, spread-eagle on the front lawn, passed out from too many tall boys. Sometimes we would see him curled up in the ditch from the top steps of the school bus as we were exiting, home for the evening. I often wondered how he had made it to the ditch and figured that he had either rolled his way down there or had been hiding from any number of his imaginary enemies and had simply drifted off to sleep.

Beatrice hated to see her father a stumbling-down, belligerent drunk.

Between Pepe and Clayton, it often felt that we were all drowning in a sea of alcohol. Almost nightly, Beatrice would grab her father by the shirt collar and haul him back into the house just before dark. Clayton had no respect for Pepe, as he thought it just awful that Pepe allowed Beatrice to drag him around the yard like a farm animal. It would have been justified if Pepe would have flattened Beatrice the first time she connected her hand to the back of his shirt collar. Clayton would have understood. Right or wrong, Pepe just stared at Beatrice all the while cursing at the air in his heavy French accent.

"Just a pussy, an old fucking foreign pussy!" Clayton would holler and bang his fist on anything nearby worthy of good sound effects.

Pepe began to take a particular interest in Sadie, who had developed full breasts that were irresistible to dear old granddad. Rubbing up against Sadie every chance he got, Pepe longed to take it a step further in his back bedroom with "that girl." Fortunately, that girl was not only a lot stronger than a fall-down drunk but a hell of a lot smarter too. Sadie knew to keep her distance and administer any payback such that it wasn't obvious to Beatrice and Clayton.

Pepe got the silent treatment on a regular basis, which simply meant we silently spit on his food, burned his toast, and cranked up our music as loud as it could go outside of his bedroom door whenever Beatrice and Clayton were off hammering nails and out of hearing distance. Silent also meant that we chose not to hear a damn thing that crazy old coot said, especially if it meant serving his needs.

When Beatrice wasn't dragging around Pepe, Clayton discovered that she was quite handy with a hammer. Although most of the heavy work of laying floors and raising walls was being done by outside help, there was still plenty more to do when the hired help went home at night. For each nail driven by Beatrice, it was one less that they would have to pay someone else to do. Most of the outside of the store was finished with the exception of a few coats of paint just short of two months after the cement for the cellar floor had been poured. Living on savings, hauling logs would have to wait until the open sign went up on the big front windows Clayton had been measuring out.

After a long day of two-by-fours, Clayton found that drinking beers and shooting the shit with Pepe was becoming more of a chore and less tolerable.

It had been too long since Clayton had made time for any fun, too long since he had sorted out any bastards or made any impromptu trips to the woods for pleasure. Even though Clayton's body was worn out from all of the physicalness of his day, his brain was amped, bored, and needing a release. Clayton was looking forward to using Rica's viciousness to his advantage. He knew Rica was a real scrapper, and it was now time for Rica to earn his keep.

"If the bums down the back road try to help themselves to my property during the night, Rica will take their fucking heads right off, all legal like. Maybe the same sons of a bitch that took my hunting dog will come back for another hand out and find themselves pulling back a stub instead." Clayton's thoughts were putting a smile on his face. He could feel his brain engaged, eager and hungry for more.

Chico had been Clayton's favorite hunting dog and one that he had kept tied up in the field a distance away from the house. Most of the time, forgotten other than the single daily trip made in his direction for mealtime, the damn dog spent his days barking and barking out of boredom. The far and few times Clayton ever took him out rabbit hunting, it was always a toss-up as to whether he would come back with a rabbit or some cat that happened to be in the wrong place at the wrong time. Either way, it made no difference to Clayton as "dead was dead." In fact, it gave Clayton great satisfaction wondering if someone would be out looking for his or her cat that would find itself dangling half dead out of the mouth of his favorite hunting dog.

Had it not been for mealtime, it might have been months before anyone realized that the links of chain no longer contained a dog at the end of it.

Chico had not slipped his collar, but by the looks of it, someone had helped themselves to one loud, barking miserable dog.

Of course, being boss, it was up to Clayton to make sure that Rica was ready to attack when necessary. Without the proper training, he might just back down on account of all the unnecessary attention his worthless daughters had been giving that dog. Rica might have turned into some kind of queer dog with no balls to fight with. It was time to right any wrongs and show Rica how to fight a real man's fight.

With a handful of rubber bands already set out on the table, Clayton went out back to retrieve Rica from his chain. Rica was not used to walks and had never been in the house, so he began to tug on the short rope in Clayton's hand with all of his might. Clayton appreciated that Rica was trying to give him a hard time, and with much satisfaction, Clayton gave a solid kick to poor Rica's underbelly, sending him sailing through the air. Rica was much more complacent after that.

Clayton called me to the kitchen, as all good things, according to Clayton, should be witnessed by someone likely to be scarred deeply by them. He was going to toughen me up right along with the dog I had tried to befriend.

"The trick is to snap him real hard on the tip of his nose to get his attention. If he yelps, immediately snap him even harder. The trick is to get him to snap at your hand," Clayton continued, feeling like some kind of big-shot, abusing a helpless dog.

"Once he can't take the pain any more, the stupid son of a bitch will snap back. When he does, he will get a little piece of dry dog food as a reward. Soon he will catch on that he needs to fight back. Next, I'll yell out a catch phrase, a word, like 'Sirrrr …' when I snap him so he will associate pain and fierceness whenever he hears that word. Pretty clever of me to think that one up, just in case I can't hit him when I need him to attack somebody. Next, I will cuff him hard a couple of times on the snout until he begins to growl. When he does, that will earn him another piece of food. He must always think that a raised hand around him means to attack or be beaten. Keep him hungry and you can keep him ready to bite, to fight back."

My head felt like it was going to explode. There was nothing I could do but stare with a painted look of false agreement smeared on my face. Right in front of my eyes, he was beating the spirit right out of poor Rica, making him take it like a man. Clayton was creating his very own living, breathing weapon of teeth, and there was nothing that I could do to stop him. I wish I had unhooked that collar and let this poor creature run free the day I set eyes on him in our backyard.

It wasn't long before Rica got the message that dinner was served only when he proved his worth. In return, Rica got to spend time in the house whenever Clayton grew tired of Pepe's stories. Being a drunk who liked to talk with his hands, Pepe's interactions with Rica became a new source of wicked entertainment for a very cruel Clayton. Rica would growl, attack, and clamp down on Pepe's arm, sometimes drawing blood in the process.

Pepe would scream, and Clayton would come in acting like the hero and save Pepe from further attack until the next time. Pepe never caught on that raised arms triggered the excitement, and Clayton never lost his enthusiasm or lust for watching the show he created in his own kitchen.

Chapter 58

PACKAGED FOOD

Summer was already in full throttle, and I had put some impressive mileage on the garden hoe. Across the field, Beatrice busied herself preparing the store for opening day. While the last coat of salmon-colored paint dried on the outer walls, Sadie, as instructed, methodically stocked the shelves with dry goods and canned goods, making sure to label each one carefully with the selling price, which Beatrice had handwritten on a steno pad.

As Sadie ripped open cardboard case after case, Clayton had all he could do not to pop her in the mouth for her noise, which made his teeth go on edge.

He decided his satisfaction would be better spent popping the top from a beer bottle instead, and the wash of the brew helped to settle his nerves from the fleechers that had been kicked up liked a sandstorm, feeling like grit between his gums.

Fleechers was a word made up by Clayton. It would be many years before any of us ever realized that Mr. Webster's Dictionary had never heard of such things. Not that any of us would have ever challenged Clayton on the subject anyway. Fleechers were also not distant cousins to the beloved Sneetches that frolicked and played with Dr. Seuss. No, Fleechers came calling whenever paper, magazines, or the dreaded cardboard, now lying at Sadie's feet, started rubbing, rustling, or connecting together. All and all, it was a Clayton original and his way of explaining the fingernails-on-a-chalkboard effect. It was also safe to say that Clayton gave both Sadie and me the fleechers whenever we found him in hearing or hitting distance.

Outdoors, the dusty, dirt parking lot had its share of every possible size and color delivery vehicle all trying to muscle their way into limited parking.

Dairy trucks, bread trucks, gas tanks on wheels—regular and the new unleaded—and, of course, the wonderful soda man with his rows and rows of delectable sweetness all stored away in glass bottles. Of course, the trucks that managed to win the closest parking were the multiple beer trucks petitioning for parking space ready to haul their dollies loaded with at least a dozen or so of Clayton's favorite flavors.

Being temporarily banished from the store, accused of being underfoot, I found my way back to the safety of the path cut through the field. Finding a comfortable spot to sit within the high weeds and tall grass, I settled in to watch the day's commotion, which played out about fifty yards away. Beatrice was a comical sight, strutting around like a barker at a carnival, the pockets of her worn shift dress bursting at the seams with cash money ready to be used to pay all the drivers for their goods. She intended to set up lines of credit for future deliveries, but her main focus that day would simply be getting her shelves stocked. Waving around cash money was the way to do it and fast.

At nine years old, my specialty was still squashing potato bugs and battling with the ragweed that always put up a fierce fight for space between the narrow rows of vegetables. Over the years, as I continued to grow, so did the size of the gardens that seemed to take over our two-acre plot of land. Now, staring out at the piece of land that would never hold rows of corn and cucumbers, I was somewhat relieved for the novelty of today's chaos.

Since morning, we had been on the receiving end of Clayton's latest threats at least a dozen times. Wielding hefty threats of physical pain if we disobeyed, Clayton wanted to make sure that we understood without any doubt we were never to touch any of the inventories available to cash-paying customers. The threat was all inclusive, though issued while he was wagging an index finger in my face. His threat included the beautiful penny candy that cast their reflections on the shiny new glass case that held at least ten dollars' worth of those wrapped treasures. As if recorded and looped on a cassette tape with the stop button jammed, Clayton ranted on and on, preaching that he knew how to deal with thieves and criminals. His beating would come swift and without remorse if he found out we consumed any of his store-bought goods.

Outside of the cartons of milk purchased after the goat died, the weekly brown paper bag overflowing with day-old bread and the occasional dented can of mackerel marked on clearance from the Grand Union, our bounty or lack thereof consisted of whatever Clayton had jotted down and approved of in the big book of rules.

"If we grew it, we could eat it. If we killed it, it would eventually end up on the supper table. If it was freezer burned and buried in the deep freeze, we could thaw it out. If sealed below wax in the menagerie of dusty canning jars, it was ours to enjoy. If green with mold and from the dirty potato bin stored in the basement, we could peel down to the less-than-rotten part. Of course, for dessert, there was always the half a dozen or so burlap sacks that smelled of mildew and contained nothing less than a zillion or more beechnuts or butternuts, ours just for the cracking."

Occasionally, as if baiting a mousetrap, Beatrice would come home with the most beautiful package birthday cake from the day-old bakery. Though it would be no one's birthday, it was indeed a special occasion, as Sadie and I licked away all of the glorious butter-cream frosting until our bellies ached and all remaining cake crumbs had been consumed. Nothing was ever free, and butter-cream frosting was no exception—whether our payback was to lie with our father, entertaining him until he finally fell into a deep sleep so Beatrice could sneak off into town, or something equally awful.

Somehow the beautifully packaged food in all of its glory, wrapped in every size and color of paper, plastic, or tin, was off limits. Did God know that we hadn't made the cut? Did he know that we were surrounded by all this food yet still hungry? Like sailors washed out to sea, dying of thirst, we too saw the irony all around us.

As the last of the delivery trucks pulled away, Beatrice looked around, making sure there were no loose ends to attend to. It was time to start the big day. Clayton's corner store was now officially ready for business.

Compliments of the wholesale cigarette company that Beatrice had paid a small fortune to, the open sign was a beauty. In bright red and yellow tubes of glowing light, the words *OPEN* came alive, reflecting off the gigantic pane of glass. Across from the window and into the other matching plate of glass was another impressive sign and Clayton's favorite. Compliments of Piels, flashing in neon, cobalt-blue lettering was "COLD BEER." It was now official; Clayton was a community businessman.

Chapter 59

THE MAN IN THE BLUE POLYESTER PANTS

I had never heard such a sound, such noise coming from the woods surrounding the gardens. At first, trying to make sense of it, I began to compare it to other sounds that I had heard in the past. Maybe it was a train off in the distance, yet I knew there were no tracks. Maybe it was a pack of older male coyotes with deep, baritone voices? As I looked up midswing of my hoe, I saw the first one. As the width of its mane broke through the tree line, I began to see others traveling toward me—large, intimidating creatures walking steadily, stealthily in my direction, forming an impassible line as they traveled. As I stood frozen, trying to wrap my mind around the impossible, trying to find the words to explain the unexplainable, two of the beasts broke rank and trailed off in the direction of Ray's shack.

At first, the screams coming from my throat did not seem like my own. How could this be so? Running toward the back porch, my legs felt warm, heavy, and as if they didn't belong to me. *Run, damn you! Move faster, faster!* I commanded of them.

The ground beneath the beasts' steps rumbled, shaking from the weight of their muscular bodies. Closer, closer, they came all the while, calling out to one another through loud, deep chest roars. Their pace was well attended to, with not one creature a pace ahead of the next. They were closing in, closing in on what or whom?

As I leaped up onto the porch, I threw open the door, allowing it to slam behind me. A simple hook would keep the door shut but never the beast out. Where would I run? Trapped behind rotten wood, I would have nothing more than to wait for my imminent end, my death. The beasts had come; they had found us.

Below my own feet, I could feel their vibration as in unison, they began to circle the house. Remaining in tight groups of no more than three or four in a circle, they were on the move, fanning out, making the circle wider and wider. Visibly shaken, I crawled to my bedroom window and carefully peered out, unprepared for the dark eyes of the beast staring back at me from no more than three feet away. The inner circle of brawny flesh so near, so close, that between the simple walls and them, I could clearly hear the raspiness of their low grunts. Was God responsible for bringing the lions? Was God angry?

The sudden swooshing sound I felt in my head made my ears pop.

Groggily, I raised my head, preparing for the worst. Darkness was there to greet me instead of the lions that I so feared. Another powerful nightmare had come and gone, this time leaving me with an incredible headache in its quake. Another close call with yet another set of nature's creatures.

Nightmares were as much a part of me as I was my miserable circumstances. Panic had paid me another visit, and it was time to get up and prepare for whatever misery was assigned to my wakening day.

The house seemed oddly quiet. Usually by six thirty, Ray was down from his little shack in the cornfield and would be sitting on his plastic trash-bag-wrapped chair, clutching a cup of instant coffee in the only mug reserved for his use, keeping his hands warm while Clayton and Beatrice went about their business of getting the day started. Being a school day, I expected to feel the springs above my head creak any minute with yet another member of the Clayton household coming to life. Sitting up and looking upward, I noticed that Sadie was no longer above, her bed already made up.

"No school today!" Beatrice hollered from the kitchen. "Doesn't mean you can sleep all day, though. Get up and find some chores or something."

Where some kids might be ecstatic that school was cancelled because of inclement weather, finding themselves all bundled up and playing for the day in the foot of ice and snow that blanketed outside, I was completely terrified. No school would mean another day of feeling like a hostage waiting for Clayton to boil over with restlessness. I could feel another dangerous day evolving, turning the clear sky outside my window an eerie gray.

It had taken Beatrice all of a week to decide that tending to the store was hard work. Once the newness had worn off, she decided that Sadie was old enough to run the store whenever she wasn't attending high school. Making the store Sadie's new home away from home, Beatrice found that she could endure the store's long hours of 7:00 a.m. to 10:00 p.m. if she could spend the better part of that day in the comforts of her favorite chair. At home, Beatrice, positioned in her sitting spot, could see the store parking lot clearly from across the field. Big brother would be watching, except it would be mother instead.

Looking around the house, I knew it would be difficult to find chores when most of what I knew had since been buried under a foot or two of snow. Feeling the pressure building inside of me, similar to the cooker that was now jetting out steam on the front gas burner in the kitchen, I knew I needed to act fast. Become scarce or busy, there weren't any other options.

Hesitantly, I asked Beatrice if I could go make myself useful at the store, helping Sadie keep the shelves and coolers stocked.

"You'll have to walk the road to the store, the plow just came through and buried up the path in the field. Don't let your father catch you walking the roads. Make yourself useful and go dust some cans."

Beatrice wouldn't take responsibility if I ended up caught by Clayton for walking out on the road, but unless I sprouted wings, I damn sure wasn't going to be able to fly there.

Without my own set of winter boots, I had to make do with the knee-high rubber work boots that had been handed down from either Curtis or Tony.

Any leftover footwear that wasn't piled in a cardboard box outside of the cellar door was left to hang by its shoestrings on the wall above the steps leading down to the floor of the cellar. With my heaviest coat already zipped up to my neck, I proceeded to open the door to the cellar and step down the couple of steps required where I could then reach the pull switch from the free-standing sixty-watt light bulb attached by an electrical cord.

As I reached for the switch that cast a thin glow of light to the bottom of the stairs below, I saw him. His body was slender, almost petite in size.

Facing away from the stairs, he held his stomach with his arms, arms that were wet from the standing water in the cellar. His knees were drawn up toward his waist as his navy-colored polyester pants were also wet and stained with a dark patch of what must have been blood or urine. On his narrow shoulders, the wet, formerly white button-down dress shirt hugged his skin. The old brown buckled ankle boots he wore with no socks underneath were splotched from the wetness that was slowly being absorbed through its hide. Although his back was to me, pressed up against the last stair, I could see his thick black wavy hair, appearing wet with clumps of hair matted together.

All alone he lay there, discarded like trash, dumped into the muck that covered that filthy, dank cellar floor. I watched for a moment, hoping that I could see movement, not that I would know what to do if I did. Even with my limited view, I could tell that all movement had likely ceased hours before I visited the cellar in hopes of finding only some warm boots.

I knew nothing of the young man who had finished out his life in the worst of places. How had he come by? I ached inside, knowing that the man lying deceased would be better remembered for his death than the life he led before evilness had scooped him up.

There are some things in life that you can never quite recover from, pain that will radiate so deep, so damaging, that like the rocks on the path to normal, passage truly does become a piece of oneself to bleed out, to be left aside forever. This would be one of those times. Healing would never come; it simply could not.

Refocusing, I grabbed the boots, yanking heavily on the laces, freeing them from the wall. After stumbling up the couple steps, I shut the cellar door with a noticeable thud. Quickly looking away from images too horrible to comprehend, I turned around to find Beatrice staring at me in the hallway with a harsh expression on her face.

"What are you doing in the cellar? Stay the hell away from it and get your ass to the store like I told you. What do you think you saw down there, huh?"

"I found the boots I was looking for; that's all," I managed to spit out, using intelligent words between the enormous smile that I had formed on my face, reserved for emergency purposes similar to the one I felt pushed into now.

Unsure as to whether I would make it out the front door before some sort of retaliation came my way, I walked thickly to the door, preparing within for whatever might strike when my back was turned. Surprisingly, it was the northern winds on my face that gave me first notification that I was going to be spared, as least for the time being. Next step would be to think, review, and connect or disconnect, whichever came first.

It wasn't that I hadn't heard the cellar door open before. I had heard it many times over the course of my life. Sometimes I had even heard the hard thud of steps connecting with heavy objects, followed by the door closing and lighter steps walking through the hallway shortly afterward. Up until then, I had only dealt with the ghosts of Clayton's departed victims. Seeing human flesh, watching life drain, was altogether a different story.

As I walked numbly through the snow, finally reaching the single step that connected with the floorboards of the store, I noticed that the salmon-colored matching tile, wet with slush and mud, had already become chipped.

Ridiculously, I focused on how mad Beatrice would be once she noticed that her floor had been carelessly treated and already damaged. Taking that final step into the store, warm with electric heat, I knew Sadie did not deserve to suffer with me. She would never need to know. Why should she?

Reaching out, I found my fingers and wrapped them tightly between silver metal rungs of the store rack nearest to the front door. Between rows of chips, my fingers held on to the rungs as it served as my anchor. I could feel myself disconnecting, half remaining a broken, empty shell while the other half of my psyche faded before me, also broken and damaged and drifting away. I watched as my reflection stood before me. With my free hand, I reached out, trying to make contact, hoping to be whole again, needing to be whole again. I had to reconnect; I had come too far to surrender now.

"I will make a trade with you," an unfamiliar voice in the nothingness called out. "Your life with no more pain. I will take over, and you may go. Go meet your other half and say good-bye forever." A voice thick with the scent, the pungency of the dark, dank cellar played in my nostrils and in my eardrums.

I would never allow evil to serve as my mentor, my guide. I began to pray, hoping Sadie could not hear, couldn't see the conflict and the commotion going on inside of me. Time passed slowly, eventually finding my fingers letting go of the metal rack. I had survived, feeling the sting, the familiarity of loss reenter my body. In reconnecting with humanity, another small piece of me, a part of innocence no longer intact, said good-bye. Another scar was etched deeply within my heart, another thought to be erased.

"Normal" began to feel like a destination far, far away, an unreachable place where forgotten children like us could never be granted passage. It was my greatest desire and yet my greatest fear. There was nothing I wanted more.

"Dear God, please help me to remain normal in all my despair."

Methodically, I ran the feather duster over the cans, interacting with Sadie superficially. I was glad for the distraction. As morning passed, I knew soon enough that Beatrice would call for me to return home. Clayton wouldn't allow his property to be out gallivanting for long, even if he knew I was working in his store. As expected, the phone call from Beatrice came shortly after the noon hour. Walking through the snowdrifts that had replaced the narrow path in the field, I began preparing for the best acting performance yet.

Clayton must have been out in his truck earlier in the day, as the driveway showed tire tracks embedded in the snow. Walking in through the kitchen, I noticed his boots sitting near the woodstove drying, still wet from the wintry weather. Obviously, he hadn't been home long. Making my arrival known, I casually walked into the living room where Beatrice and Clayton sat with large bowls of soup and potted meat sandwiches on their television trays. The noon hour was dinnertime for the Clayton twosome.

With precision and perfection, my acting performance would have to be convincing if I wanted to remain alive and safe. Gingerly, I remarked how delicious the soup smelled and how glad I was to be back home out of the weather. Beatrice and Clayton threw a noticeable glance at each other, pausing for a moment before returning to their big bowl of greasy broth.

The look on their faces softened, satisfied that I was unaware of their little secret.

Pretending to be hungry, I began making the motions of working the soup ladle, filling my bowl with air. "Delicious," I repeated to no one in particular as I carried the empty bowl and spoon to my bedroom to think.

Proud of my performance, I knew that my deception would give me at least an hour of alone time before either of them would come barging in, demanding to know why I was hiding from them.

I knew that the man who had lain on the cellar floor directly below my own bedroom's floorboards had probably been removed. Even with the roads unfit for travel, Clayton had a need, a drive, to complete his circle of horror. Lying on the bed deep in thought, I felt my eyes drift to the wall across from me. Staring at the blank wall, I began to wonder why so much evil was allowed to walk freely, destroying people along the way. As I thought, I noticed that the wall began to form large droplets of moisture, of water.

The wall being an inner wall was protected from the harsh temperatures outside. I had never seen droplets of water before on any walls. Standing up, I wondered if it was condensation, yet none of the other walls showed such moisture.

Taking a closer look, I watched droplets of water coming up from below the wall's surface, forming even larger droplets of water that ran down the length of the wall toward the floor. As I watched, I realized with astonishment that the wall appeared to be crying. Without hesitation, I turned and leaned back into the wall with my hands outstretched, feeling the tears run down my own body toward the floor. I began to weep silently, flushing the pain out, crying with the wall as we became one. I wasn't alone in my anguish; the walls felt the pain too. They knew of the others, and for this moment in my life, we were mourning those lost. Someone had to.

Chapter 60

APONI

Out of the impossible, a butterfly emerges.

Sadie's life began with the opening of the store. Had there been a way, she never would have come home again. The store was her refuge, her strand of humanity that stretched to accommodate her broken heart. Although she worked hard taking care of the business, in doing so, she slowly became whole, slowly learned how to smile. Being with people and not only monsters, Sadie began to see that the future held hope. It would be a long time, however, before she would trust anyone. But hope has a way of paving a path of illumination, eventually revealing to her that in time, in forgiveness, she would find trust.

Being the middle child would have come with the standard, ordinary middle-child issues had we been an ordinary family. Unfortunately, with our given circumstances, Sadie became not only the child to slip through the cracks but also the child picked on, chosen to take the brunt of the harshest physical abuse. All of the day's pent-up rage would first be taken out on Sadie, then trickle down to me, thereafter. Further degrading Sadie, Clayton's constant lewdness included wagging his tongue at her after a particularly hard shove or a backhander just so she would know that he still found her sexually attractive even if she was all bruised up.

At three years old, Sadie began her education early. With an old chalkboard and a box of white chalk, Sadie was taught every sexual term, word, and phrase that had ever come out of a bottom-rung whorehouse.

Clayton, always looking for humor in the sickest of ways, watched as his oldest daughter taught Sadie the ways of the English language, all the while fondling himself in the background. Sadie would also experience some of the words she was required to spell. Though her mind drifted off to safety, her body remained in the lesson.

With six years apart in age, I became Sadie's responsibility early on, a task that she would have liked to have forfeited the first time she tried to discipline me. Already filled with pain and rage, I could kick like a donkey, back pressed to the dirty living room floor. She wouldn't know that the kicks were never meant for her, yet she was the one who received them full force. I spent my fair share of time in the corner as punishment; Sadie tried to do her part in giving me a normal, structured childhood.

Unfortunately, regardless of her heartfelt efforts, there still was nothing normal about our childhood for either of us.

We were sisters who became friends even though Clayton had forbidden it. Sadie was a loner, smart enough to know that outside friendships couldn't be nurtured, couldn't be reciprocated. She valued her time watching out for her younger sister perhaps in ways she had once longed for, for herself. With fields and woods just outside of our property line, Sadie and I would walk for hours, all the while talking about silliness and things we couldn't share at home. The walks were precious to Sadie, as out in the fields, away from home, she didn't have to disappear, didn't have to be invisible.

Sadie trusted me even though to her, trust took a life of its own, leering at her like a villain in the darkness, waiting to punish her. Like a rubber band, I stretched her trust boundaries and hurt her, though my intentions didn't come out of maliciousness. Sadly, Clayton's need for a practical joke had found its way to me. While I didn't intend on doing harm, I hadn't yet understood that getting a laugh shouldn't be at someone else's expense.

Playing a game of blind man's bluff one afternoon, just the two of us, Sadie put her trust in me to guide her safely. With her eyes covered with a blindfold, it was up to me to direct her through an obstacle course that finished in front of the house; it was a chance to earn her trust, to let her know I had her back.

Being clever, waiting for the perfect practical joke, I began to watch Ray scooping buckets of sewage from the septic tank, a task Clayton had given him so the tank wouldn't have to be pumped. Ray had been throwing our human waste all over the back gardens and into the previously dried-up swamp now thick with bucket loads of stench. While directing Sadie around the yard, as an awful prank, I led her, blindfold intact, to the middle of the sewage swamp. She had trusted me to do no harm, but when she took her blindfold off, she didn't laugh. Trust wouldn't come out to play again for a very long while.

Sadie would be the last of the siblings who would feel the sting of the belt if her grades fell below what Clayton deemed her capable of getting.

Regardless of the trauma at home and the extensive chores, Sadie was to keep all A's and B's. Homework did not become a government conspiracy that stole students from their parents until Sadie was out of the nest and I was the only one left.

As Sadie grew into a teenager, she would tuck away any money she received so she could save up for clothes, namely coveted bodysuits. In the 1970s, all the girls were wearing them. They were the latest fashion, comprised of a pretty blouse complete with snaps that would connect in the crotch area, keeping the blouse permanently and securely tucked in. Sadie had so few nice things to wear, and bodysuits made her feel special and pretty. With her long, dark hair parted neatly down the center, her blueberry-colored eyes wide and alluring, her signature dark shoelace wrapped around her neck as jewelry, the bodysuit worn with jeans added the final touches to an already beautiful girl.

It didn't escape Beatrice's attention that Sadie liked the way she looked as she began to turn into a young woman. Pride and dignity were traits that were despised by both Beatrice and Clayton. Pride would breed independence, and that in itself would threaten to undermine all the evil doings and destruction that Beatrice and Clayton thrived on behind everyone's backs. Methodically, Beatrice would spend the next few years trying to destroy Sadie's spirit completely.

All teenagers, regardless of background, have a need to rebel. Sadie was no exception, though she had a lot more to lose from it if caught. Watching the regular customers intensely, Sadie recognized that most of them smoked cigarettes. Regulars would stop by for gas and a pack of cigarettes, and the ones Sadie knew best, she began to ask for cigarettes from. Smoking was the one thing that Sadie could do that made her feel in charge of herself. She had even gone so far as to purchase packs of her own menthol cigarettes, which she stashed up on top of the soda and beer coolers.

Clayton, either chewing tobacco, smoking his pipe, rolling his own cigarettes—both the legal kind and the not-so-legal kind—believed that all men should smoke or chew. Beatrice, however, was not allowed to smoke, as being female, it went against Clayton's authority. Beatrice didn't always placate Clayton on his terms, and she was known to puff on a pack of Salem cigarettes whenever she felt strong enough to take a beating or mad enough that she didn't care about the outcome. Clayton would have never dreamed that his female property, namely Sadie, would have the audacity to defy him in that way.

The day Sadie's world changed, she had been enjoying a cigarette in between customers at the store. Beatrice and Clayton were accounted for, as they had left for the hill, their favorite wood lot, just an hour prior. Hoping to attract some bucks for hunting season, Clayton was checking his salt licks on a regular basis, both early morning and at dusk. Ray, always on the lookout for a beer, had been forbidden to go to the store, as any beer purchase had to be cleared through Clayton first. Even though Clayton was an alcoholic himself, it gave him great satisfaction to watch Ray suffer with his addiction, withholding what he needed until Clayton was good and ready.

Ray, also sensing his window of opportunity and few minutes of freedom, had sprinted through the field, finding a spot to duck behind once he came to the back side of the store. Even with Clayton gone, there was always the risk of being caught and a paranoia that came from multiple beatings. Making that final dart to the front door, Ray ran right smack into the smoke from Sadie's cigarette.

I believe Ray only ratted Sadie out because he knew that all alone in the woods with Clayton would be a very dangerous place to be caught in a lie.

However it came up, the next day, while working in the woods, Clayton asked and Ray confirmed, Sadie was smoking.

I knew the moment I got off the school bus and entered the house that something was extremely wrong. Beatrice met me at the door and in a low hiss told me that I had three minutes to feed all the goddamn animals and get my ass back into the house, her words. Three minutes sounds like a short time, but when you are waiting to see if you will live or die, it actually becomes quite a long bit of time to wait for the answer. Swiftly I threw grain and water at the dogs, pigs, and chickens and ran up the back steps back to the living room where Beatrice was methodically pulling her hair out strand by strand.

"Your father is going to kill your sister, and when he is done, he is going to come home and kill you." Beatrice spoke very matter-of-factly. "You sit your ass down in that chair until he gets home and don't move a muscle."

I methodically watched the clock over the television. In fact, from three thirty in the afternoon going forward, I did nothing but stare at the big hand, watching it move down and around the numbers for nearly two hours. Staring at the clock helped me to fixate, slow my breathing, contain my fear, say a few Hail Marys, and prepare to die, in case the threats were real this time. As the clock reached six, I knew that craziness would soon arrive home in his old truck at just about any minute.

As I was finishing the last of my prayers, Beatrice came out of her bedroom, carrying a plastic shopping bag from the department store in town.

Slowly she took out a white bodysuit, new with the tags still attached. I knew that Sadie had given Beatrice money earlier in the week to pick up a bodysuit for her while Beatrice was out shopping. It seemed a peculiar time for Beatrice to be handling the blouse unless she was intending to bury Sadie in it. With a smug look on her face, Beatrice turned away and out the door heading to the store where Sadie, completely oblivious to the dangers, was working the cash register. The nightmare was fixing to unfold.

Sadie hadn't seen it coming. Beatrice seemed in a good enough mood as she relieved Sadie from the cash register, summoning her to go put on the new bodysuit that she had picked up for her earlier in the day. Lying that she wanted to make sure that it fit, Beatrice waited with anticipation for Sadie to come out from the bathroom, waiting to see that prideful look on her face that she hated so much.

Clayton remained out of sight just outside the front door until the last of the customers pulled out of the parking lot. Then and only then did he come through the door to the delight of Beatrice and to the detriment of poor Sadie.

The first blow caught Sadie on the side of her head, tearing the retina in her right eye. Temporarily left dazed and confused from the force of the impact, Sadie tried to steady herself, blinking with the eye that showed her nothing but bright, disorienting light. Grabbing the back of Sadie's thick dark hair, making sure to rip some out in the process, Clayton began to drag Sadie home through the path in the field.

Clayton laughed as he ripped the brand-new white bodysuit right off Sadie's back. Like Beatrice, he had been looking forward to this. Once the last of Sadie's clothing had been torn away, Clayton grabbed the thick leather belt from the loops of Sadie's own pants, which had been tossed onto the bedroom floor.

There are monsters, and then there are monsters even to monsters. Clayton was the latter. With not the leather strap but the large, thick metal buckle, Clayton began striking Sadie over and over, leaving deep, distinctive buckle tracks sliced into her skin. Sadie slid in and out of consciousness as

Clayton continued to upright her, demanding that she remain awake for the duration of her beating. After several minutes of vicious and violent blows from the belt, Clayton stopped. Even in his adrenaline-induced rage, he had realized that a dead daughter wouldn't be as rewarding, as gratifying, as the pleasures he would reap seeing the fear in Sadie's eyes again and again for weeks to come. Even with his lust to kill, to finish what he started, he restrained himself from the climax. After all, his own cleverness was what had made him so unstoppable, completely invincible all these years.

Clayton, being quite pleased with his performance, his inner beast relaxed and well exercised, left Sadie slumped on the floor in his bedroom. It would be time to celebrate with some brandy. After all, he had pinned his opponent after only a few rounds!

Sadie eventually came out of the bedroom, covering herself with the torn remains of her clothes. She knew that once she left that bedroom, she would have to return to the Sadie who didn't show grudges, didn't cry, wouldn't pout or feel sorry for herself. In fact, she would be required to show no emotion at all. She was relieved from her store duties for the one night, though it was the only place she longed to be. Later, she would walk Rica up to the store and deposit him inside to watch over the place at closing time. Her body red and swollen from the assault would barely accept clothes over her welts, bruises, and cuts. The next day, Beatrice would write her a two-line note for school, telling them that Sadie wouldn't be in gym class until further notice. As usual, no one would bat an eye, no one cared to question why.

Being in shock is too ambiguous to describe the war that I had raging in my head. I do not remember what happened next as I watched helplessly as Sadie was dragged to Clayton's bedroom. There are times when one simply cannot stay inside the body one finds no safety in, times like this one where the only place safe to hide is no actual place at all. Running to the far recesses of my mind, my only memory would be sitting with my hands over my head and my knees drawn tightly to my chin. Time stood still and became soundless, surreal. Another piece of me would have to be left to pay the toll upon my return.

Sadie returned to the store directly after school the next day. While she relieved Mother from her duties, Sadie gazed out into the field, watching the back of the woman who had betrayed her so easily walking away. Lighting up a menthol cigarette as she watched, she sucked in the smoke deeply, hoping that when she exhaled, the pain from welts too numerous to count wouldn't make her wince inside.

Chapter 61

BLACK AND WHITE AND WEDDING BELLS

Seasons passed with time ticking away in its usual fashion. Home life remained a colossus of fear and uncertainty, yet like the ebb and flow of the tides, the store ensured a flow of hope and change in our day-to-day living.

Happiness, though confusing at first, still came, bringing with it bite-size morsels of fun and laughter. The store was teaching us how to feel, how to be more than just shadows.

Sadie's time was coming to an end as the sand in her hourglass was emptying into adulthood, into freedom. Soon Sadie would be making her exit. I, however, knew that in only a few short months, the ghosts in the house would have me all to themselves. Last man standing so to speak, last one left to face the cellar, and worst, last child to leave.

Instead of green grass and jellybeans, the week of Easter came with yet another set of surprises. Though the ground was ready to be tilled and the indoor tomato plants were ripe for transplanting out of doors, a hell of a snowstorm hit the North Country. While not uncommon to see snow flurries even as late as April, most of those threats came with virtually no accumulation to speak of. This two feet of inconvenience not only hit unexpectedly, finding the Clayton household with virtually no cut wood left for the stoves but also a cold body waiting to be discovered in the back bedroom.

Sadie, gladly missing the breakfast ritual, had hastily put on oversized boots and made a swift exit into the early morning snow. Always prompt, she could rarely wait until seven to open the store. Lingering any longer in the house she wished to be rid of simply didn't make any sense to her. Although Beatrice was home and sitting in her favorite chair, watching the snow blow outside of her window, Pepe's breakfast would be my responsibility. Burned toast would have been fitting enough had Beatrice not been so watchful.

Even if she didn't have any use for her own father, it would still be our duty to see that he had something better to eat than what Sadie or I had.

As far as I was concerned, the back bedroom, although no bigger than a large closet, seemed cozy and safe—a haven wasted on the likes of a man who had no appreciation for others' deeds, others' sacrifices. After making my way to the door, I began to rap with the back of my knuckles, hoping to get the point across that it was time to get up. Being reminded of the simple fact that none of us ever got to sleep past six helped to intensify the already loud knocking on Pepe's door.

"Time to get up, Pepe." The tone in my voice didn't dare show the hostility that I had stuffed down, repressed over the last two years. Pepe was an unwelcome visitor, always had been. As he was not responding to his name, I opened the door and walked over to where he lay sleeping on his side.

Reaching down to shake his shoulder, I saw that his left ear was full of blood, cold and congealed, probably from a long night exposed to the cold room.

Pepe wouldn't be coming out for breakfast.

***

The funeral procession was an odd sight. Beatrice had seen to it that her bunch rode in the front car, as it had been strictly on account of her generosity and kind ways that Pepe had a place to stay in the first place. Her worthless sisters, as she repeatedly shared with anyone in hearing distance, never did their part, never offered to help with the cost or hassle of housing and feeding their alcoholic and abusive father. Now they could find their own way, their own transportation.

"Walk through the frigging snow to the funeral home if they have to."

Being happy to be back home didn't speak much for the company I kept through the whole procession. Later, between bites of potato salad and cold-cut sandwiches, I watched as Beatrice snarled and bickered back and forth with her sisters. Each decided individually that they had been the favorite daughter. Disgusted, I quietly stared at the sorry bunch, knowing my instincts had always been correct. Sharing any information about what actually happened here behind drawn shades with the likes of this selfish, horrible group would have only put Sadie and me in further danger.

Keeping quiet had been a smart decision.

Sadie quickly removed the ugly black dress that Beatrice had made from a ream of cheap material discovered once upon a time at the clearance table at the five-and-dime. Whether out of wishful thinking or sheer anger, Beatrice had thrown it together one night after a terrible fight with Clayton.

Every now and again, after one of her awful beatings, she would call us out to the living room, while Clayton remained passed out either on the bathroom floor or in the bedroom and announce that she was planning to kill herself. Much as if she were going into town for some shopping, she casually told of her plans to swallowing every last one of Clayton's remaining foil-wrapped sleeping pills. After her speech, she would pour a cup of hot tea and busy herself at the sewing machine. When she felt satisfied, usually a few hours later, there would be a couple of misshapen black shift dresses sprawled out on her chair. The dress Sadie had been wearing had been from Beatrice's clothing collection.

Throwing on a pair of threadbare jeans, Sadie headed to her sanctuary, preparing to unlock the store for business. The handwritten sign still taped to the center of the locked door was a simple one and straight to the point: "Closed. Death in the Family. Reopen Later in the Day."

Beatrice always had a knack for summing up circumstances in as few words as possible. "Out of sight, out of mind" summed up everything about the Clayton family—dressed in black by noon, forgotten by suppertime.

People were disposable, and mourning was simply for the weak of heart.

Beatrice felt time already spent for the wake and funeral was enough time allotted to the situation, enough said.

Sadie could feel her spirits lift the moment the open sign sputtered to life in the cold front window. Life as Sadie knew it would be returning to normal now. The store was her world, and she was glad for it. The sign was like turning on the light to her front porch; she was home. It was good to see familiar faces, and they seemed to appreciate Sadie as well. Some of the boys from the neighborhood enjoyed coming to the store simply to hang out. Sadie had a friendly and playful disposition, and the locals knew that she wouldn't kick them out for loitering, no matter how long they stayed.

It had been the previous summer while studying the behaviors of customers who came in to purchase ice and snacks for coveted lake trips that Sadie saw him. He was a handsome man, not much older than she. Driving a souped-up Dodge Dart, tall, dark, and handsome liked to spin his tires on the loose gravel for show. He had gotten Sadie's attention, hook, line, and sinker.

Their secret romance continued into Sadie's senior year of high school.

Catching forbidden rides home from school, Sadie knew she had found her future husband. Sadie was ready to get married; it was time to get out of Clayton's house.

Fortunately for everyone's sake, Mother Nature decided to crank up the heat out of doors and the winter wonderland turned into a wet spring practically overnight. Not wanting to waste time, I quickly moved my few belongings to the small back bedroom a little further away from the monsters down the hall. I hated leaving Sadie by herself, but it was time to take the lead. Soon it would be just me, and I needed to get used to being without Sadie. Times were changing, and loneliness would soon be only a wedding ring away.

Beatrice became indignant, making it known that I had hurt her feelings deeply for not asking for permission to switch rooms. She didn't appreciate my behavior and my arrogance, believing that I was entitled to the bedroom in the first place. After she got a good share of belittling out of her system, at my expense, she decided I could sleep there if I absolutely had to.

Unfortunately, Beatrice also decided that she couldn't be bothered to wash the sheets that Pepe had died on for the better part of two months. It was her way of getting back at me for my insolent behavior. In the interim, Pepe and I got to know each other quite well. Sleeping through the scent of BenGay, beer, and old person helped me to come to terms with the fact that I really had disliked my grandfather and he had felt the same way about me. To him, I had always been just "that girl."

Sadie wanted out—now. Unfortunately, she wouldn't be of legal age until the middle of July. She knew that asking permission to get married would be a touchy subject. Beatrice and Clayton had so much to lose with Sadie gone. She would have to word it such that it would seem that Beatrice and Clayton would come out the winners in the end. Sadie would continue to work at the store, the difference being she would no longer be a financial burden to Beatrice and Clayton. Someone else would be responsible for her upkeep and care after she was married. She would have to word things just right, so Clayton would understand.

Begrudgingly, Beatrice and Clayton agreed that Sadie could get married as long as they alone picked the wedding date. If Sadie was going to inconvenience them with a wedding, they were going to get the last laugh, come hell or high water.

Two weeks before Sadie's eighteenth birthday, picked to coincide with the start of Sadie's menstrual cycle, Sadie and her new husband were to wed.

On the morning of the wedding, Sadie worked at the store until Beatrice called her, giving the go-ahead to lock up. Cruelly, Beatrice waited until Sadie had about an hour remaining to get home, get dressed, and be at the church. Running through the front door, Sadie had hoped she could rinse off with a quick bath but found Clayton in the tub, fighting with Beatrice, who was standing on the other side of the closed door. Weddings were expensive, and Clayton was furious. It was just sinking in that he would be expected to buy drinks for the guests at the reception. Forgoing the bath, Sadie hastily put on her wedding dress all the while trying to drown out Clayton's voice, which was banging around in her head, causing a massive headache.

Making it to the church only a few minutes late, Sadie looked beautiful, even though her wedding dress was made from a simple bed sheet complete with a lace curtain wrapped around her head as a veil. In order to hold the veil in place, Clayton had come up with the brilliant idea of using an old starter rope from his chainsaw to hold the curtain from shifting off his daughter's head.

According to Clayton, I had probably been the one to encourage Sadie with all this marriage talk. For my part in the trouble, Beatrice had made certain that I had something nice to wear too. My floor-length blue shift dress came complete with white splotches of color that looked like I had stood extensively under a flock of pigeons and they had relieved themselves substantially. Effectively, we had covered the something old, something borrowed, something bizarre, and something blue. Life away from Clayton and Beatrice would be the something new, something very new—*freedom*.

After the wedding, Sadie was relieved from her duties at the store for the rest of the day. Beatrice never made it to the reception of her daughter's wedding because it just wasn't important enough to keep the store closed all day for. Needless to say, Clayton stayed, bought drinks for himself, and got completely hammered. Dancing to his favorite songs from the jukebox, Clayton decided that the first dance should be a solo production of Clayton doing the twist for all of our embarrassment. Later, after the cake was cut and Sadie and her new husband had slipped away, Sadie's new mother-in-law, still stunned over the day's events, wrapped up the remaining cake, including the top, and proceeded to take it home for safekeeping.

Well, as no good deed goes unpunished, she quickly learned the error of her ways. Beatrice, using every curse word known to man, threw an explosive temper tantrum over the phone into the ear of Sadie's new family. Somewhere between the part of the "fucking cake being stolen by white-trash thieves and bring my goddamn cake back," the line went dead. Needless to say, within the hour, Beatrice had received the rest of the wedding cake, wrapped in tinfoil, sitting on the step of her front porch.

Clayton, still drunk after his debut, saw his opportunity to get involved with all the excitement. Tossing the crushed tinfoil package in the front seat of the pickup, Clayton weaved his way to the honeymooner's new home and deposited the now-flattened cake on top of their trash cans. He would show them he didn't appreciate the trouble they had stirred up.

Soon after Clayton arrived back home, Beatrice put a handwritten sign on the front door of the store; it was a simple sign, "For Sale."

Another sibling had been declared officially dead by Clayton and Beatrice.

Chapter 62

FLYING MONKEYS

Dorothy knew that the wicked witch had cast a spell on good men, turning them into monkeys with wings. Unbinding the spell, Dorothy was able to free them forever, destroying the wicked witch in the process.

Clayton had been drinking full bottles of horse liniment ever since Pepe had gone to the other side. It was hard mistaking the smell of that foul concoction that sat front and center on the kitchen counter. Each of us knew the taste firsthand, as we had been drinking a tablespoon of it every night since we could swallow. The undeniable label, boasting a light-colored mare, teeth showing, camera ready—stupid damn horse! Liniment was designed as a rub for horses, the answer for sore muscles from the simple plow horse up to and including thoroughbreds. Guaranteed to lift the lameness from any steed.

In the middle of another Clayton revelation, liniment had been discovered. Yes, liniment, although claimed not to be fit for human consumption, was actually an elixir, bottled straight from the fountain of youth. Another well-kept government secret that Clayton had uncovered—those bastards!

Clayton, always the cautious and crafty soul, felt it necessary to test his theory on the family first. If his revelation was wrong, well, he wouldn't be the guinea pig. Surprisingly, the family didn't seem to have any ill effects from his little experiment, so liniment was the new staple in the Clayton household.

A few months had passed since Pepe's death. Beatrice's lack of empathy and remorse hadn't gone unnoticed by Clayton. In fact, she had seemed downright gleeful, forgetting the whole matter. This made Clayton very uneasy. Maybe Beatrice had plans for him? Maybe she was enjoying her new situation a little too much. A feeling of paranoia began to set in.

"Kill him and bury his body in the backyard and steal all of his money!"

Nagging thoughts that he would be next helped to fuel his evening drinking binges, sending them into overdrive.

Of course, the only actual money Clayton and Beatrice ever had was already buried out in the yard in place of Clayton. From coffee cans to mayonnaise jars, Beatrice and Clayton had a passion for packing containers with loose change, silver certificates, and anything else they deemed valuable and couldn't share or part with. Once Beatrice had set her eyes upon the commercial, gallon-sized jars of pickles, pickled eggs, and sausages from the store, she had all she could do not to fish out the contents with a pair of tongs, emptying her beloved jars for other uses.

"Burying time," a nickname I had given to their bizarre jarring rituals, happened every couple of months, give or take—sometimes more often once the ground thawed. It always started the same way. Beatrice and Clayton would begin whispering to each other like schoolchildren. Next, I would be banished off to my bedroom for the afternoon. Then, I would hear them working jars and lids on the metal kitchen table. Sometimes the sound of change could be heard rolling on the old linoleum followed by a couple, "damnits," but usually they were pretty hush-hush, busy with their work.

Occasionally, the sounds of footsteps could be heard going up and down the cellar stairs. Perhaps Clayton had hidden some cash money in the crawl space. Waiting and listening, I knew once the back door shut behind them, I would have a few minutes to sneak out of my room and hide behind the curtain to watch them dig. Their favorite hiding spot was directly below their bedroom window. Maybe they thought they could keep a better eye on their treasures from that spot. Burying time usually took about thirty minutes from start to finish and always ended with the sound of wrestling blasting from the old television in the living room, shovels put away until next time.

As we were living like paupers and surviving on a lot of mustard sandwiches, I found it hard to imagine that they had enough money to fill up even a mustard jar.

On the weekend I was to make my sacrament of Confirmation in the Catholic church, Clayton went completely nuts. Whether it was the liniment coming back to haunt him or any other number of reasons, he went completely, stark-raving mad. He was literally foaming at the mouth, crawling on all fours, growling, and snapping at the air. Clayton spent the better part of three days acting as if he were possessed. Power drinking day and night, Clayton dragged Beatrice around the house by her hair, giving her two swollen-shut black eyes and a number of bruises just by the end of the first day.

Emptying all of the contents of the refrigerator onto the kitchen floor, Clayton began smashing ketchup bottles and mustard jars against the walls with such force that the walls became dented, splattered from ceiling to baseboards. For every jar he threw, for every plastic dish of soup he threw from the ancient refrigerator, he screamed for me to get busy and clean up my mess or he would wipe up the mess with me.

Terrified, between uncontrollable tears, I cleaned up glass, food, and everything else, for the better part of three days. The knots in my stomach soon became dry heaves, my thoughts distant and cloudy.

Everything we owned, although not much, was broken, shattered. The metal kitchen table was flung upside down with its legs bent and twisted.

Each metal kitchen chair teeter-tottered from shelves or the backs of the living room furniture. Our house was a war zone with Clayton battling it out with the demons in his head. On the morning of the third day, with already two sleepless nights spent rolling oranges around the obstacle course in the living room, Beatrice demanded that I put on my Confirmation dress. It was time to make my statement to God. It was my duty to go and beg for Clayton's salvation, as it was on account of me that his soul had been offered up to the devil in the first place.

Watching Clayton on all fours, spitting tobacco juice everywhere, I truly believed that the devil she spoke of was thoroughly enjoying his performance done on our behalf. I wouldn't ask for his salvation though.

Confirmation would serve another purpose. It was going to serve as my plea, my resurrection from this hell. It was time to stand up and beg for my salvation—issue my public plea to God that he allow me to be like everyone else, to end up strong and "normal," although I still couldn't quite understand what that truly meant. Would God save another lamb from Satan?

Battered and bruised, Beatrice sat in the back pew with sunglasses on. In spite of the overcast day filled with rain, no one seemed to notice.

Staring into the faces of the good Christians who came for the show, I was astounded that not one mentioned the dark, deep circles that outlined my eyes, the eyes that had been crying for nearly forever, swollen with the redness of abuse and despair. Refusing to see the truth all around them, they stood up and clapped, and then off they went to enjoy their Sunday dinner of roast and pie while Beatrice and I headed back home. Feeling abandoned and stunned over the lack of compassion from God's flock, I hadn't asked for anything. Too lost to beg for salvation, I had said nothing. God would have to hear my pleas from the silence of my prayers instead—the prayers that I dared never say aloud.

I gathered my senses while stuffing my disappointment back within me as Beatrice put the car into park. We were home, just in time for our next beating.

Finally, as the clouds parted and the sky cleared, Clayton emerged the following Monday into the old Clayton we knew and despised. Looking around, he seemed puzzled that the house was in such disarray. Deciding that Beatrice had been neglectful and lazy over the weekend, he made a mental note to set her straight once he got home from working in the woods later in the day.

Grabbing my schoolbooks from underneath my bed, I was grateful that the long holiday weekend was over. House rule didn't allow us to dwell on anything from one day to the next. No mention of it, no memory of it. That was the mantra of my entire childhood. Now, as I stood waiting in front of our shack for the tired yellow school bus, I wondered how many other kids out there were just like me. How many had to forget? How many others lived with the devil?

Some distractions can be a welcomed sight, breaking up the monotony of life. We were about to have another one, but this time, it didn't involve Clayton. Tony had been in town after taking a couple of detours and dead-end roads along the way. College would be over for now, and desperation had sent him to his least-favorite place, back home with us—but only as a temporary stay. Tony and his latest companion, a small sheltie collie came to live with us for a couple weeks, just passing through.

Little Shammy, the collie, had never spent a night outdoors. Somehow, Tony convinced Beatrice, while she was in a good mood, I suspect, to let him hide this poor little creature in the bedroom with him. I was surprised and relieved at her unexpected generosity. I knew that our tortured German shepherds, two now, would have torn that little dog to shreds if he had been tied up with them outside. It wouldn't guarantee his safety, but it was a good start.

For two weeks, poor Shammy, scared and confused, ate away at the old carpet in Tony's room while Tony did his best to stay gone, away from the house, figuring out his life in private.

I felt sorry for the little dog, as he looked about as out of place as a king in a garbage dump. Taking care of Shammy, I was careful to keep him quiet behind the closed door. I knew Clayton would have no problem swinging the animal from the clothesline if he started getting on his nerves. Shammy and I became fast friends, up until the night that I nearly choked the life out of him.

Clayton, deciding that he wanted to get a jump on a long weekend of drinking, headed out to his favorite gay bar. Although Friday nights were usually a drink-alone-at-home event, this Friday, Clayton wanted company.

Beatrice was relieved. Able to claim a few minutes of alone time, she settled in to watch an old rerun of *The Waltons* on television. She knew that when Clayton returned, he wouldn't be alone. He always managed to bring something home, a little someone for the both of them to enjoy.

It had been dark outside for a couple of hours. Knowing that Clayton would be home soon after he found what he wanted, I hastily put the makeshift leash of clothesline rope around Shammy's neck and took him outside to do his business. After walking out the front door, I headed to the side of the house where the long grass would be inviting to a dog. A couple of feet from where I waited stood an enormous stack of structural planks, lumber that extended in length about twelve to sixteen feet and was piled at least six feet high from the ground. Clayton, deciding that he would rather build houses to rent instead of staying in the grocery business, had recently purchased enough wood to lay the foundation of his latest and greatest project.

As I turned, ready to head back inside, I felt a sudden rush of very cold air, bringing an intense chill to the summer evening. The air felt heavy, charged with static electricity, making the hair on the back of my neck stand on end. Instinctively, I looked up to where the chill had originated, just as a massive black flying creature with at least a ten-foot wingspan began to swoop up and off from the ground toward me, lifting its body up and over the pile of lumber. As it cleared the lumber pile, its hind end hit the top couple of layers of heavy planks, sending them flying lengthwise through the air as if they were as light as matchsticks.

This was not a nightmare; this was real, and I was terrified. With my heart pounding so loudly it was deafening, I snapped hard at the rope, swinging it over my head like a kite and began running as fast as my legs would take me to the front steps of the house. The last I saw of the enormous black manta-ray-shaped creature was as it flew up above my head and into the dark night sky. Clearing the steps, I rushed through the front door while trying to catch my breath, remembering only then that Shammy was still on the end of the rope.

Dazed and gasping for breath, the poor little dog began to shake and convulse. It had been only sheer luck that I hadn't snapped the poor animal's neck with the jerking motion. I began to cry, cradling the poor scared dog in my arms. Shammy would live, though it was doubtful if he would ever be normal again.

Regaining my senses, unsteadily, I walked into the living room where Beatrice sat quietly, the television now off. I didn't care how foolish I sounded; I had just witnessed the most frightening sight that I had ever believed imaginable. Even the ghosts that rattled around in the house were no comparison to this flying creature that effortlessly knocked over a thousand-pound stack of lumber. Beatrice's reaction wouldn't be so important. I just had to get the words that were screaming loudly, banging on the sides of my temples, to come out to somebody—anybody.

Beatrice listened, staring at me intensely with her deep brown eyes. The surge of adrenaline, making my legs weak, slowly began to recede but only after my third retelling. As I stammered out the words, the event seemed amazingly surreal. Trying to sound more intelligent and rational on each recollection, I really didn't want a response, just a sounding board, someone to listen. I needed to be heard to settle the intoxicating fear crawling inside of me.

Beatrice methodically reached for her hair, pulling out single strands as she always did when the cogs in her head were turning. Pausing to choose her words carefully, she looked at me, and then, in a voice barely audible, barely above a whisper, she shared, "I know exactly what you saw. I saw it too when I was a young girl out picking berries by the track."

Gathering her thoughts, Beatrice turned her head slowly from me, drifting away to the place between nothingness and emptiness. She was done with our conversation.

"Now I lay me down to sleep, I pray the Lord my soul to keep. If I should die before I wake, I pray the Lord my soul to take. God, save me from all the evil, all the darkness of this horrible house. Keep me normal in my loneliness or show me mercy and take me away now and forever. Amen."

Chapter 63

BATTEN DOWN THE HATCHES, STORMY SEAS AHEAD

Six years would be a long time to hold the beasts off. I was alone now, front and center. In some ways, life became easier. Being alone, I would have no distractions, no remaining siblings to worry about. The beasts would have no leverage. Interactions would simply come down to a push and pull, a test of wills between the three of us. No other emotions would be there to clutter up the landscape. I had a job to do, and I had six years to accomplish my goals. I would keep my eye on the prize of normalcy and the chance to be declared dead to Clayton so that I might actually live, free from harm, away from the two of them, forever.

Sadie was gone, now a married woman. Even though the store changed ownership, she kept her promise. Sadie would continue working at the store, fostering the relationships, she had built over the years, keeping a close eye on her little sister. This new boss didn't rip bodysuits from her back, and she didn't have to be worried for her life. He was no Clayton.

Beatrice carried a grudge like a pitchfork, wielding it through the air, hoping to connect with anything, anyone. It made no difference to Beatrice that Sadie stayed close by because she had left in the first place. Beatrice and Clayton added a new rule to the master book—a rule I was to strictly obey or suffer dire consequences.

"Stay the hell away from your sister. She is married now, and she belongs to her new husband."

Already having forewarned me a number of times, Clayton continued his daily threats, listing the consequences I would face if I didn't "stay the hell away from Sadie." Repeatedly, I was reminded that Sadie's husband didn't need a tramp like me hanging around his castle, period! I would be nothing more than a distraction in their marriage, and Clayton would not allow it.

My role in my sister's adult life, or lack thereof, was not the only entry and modification made in the big book of rules. Homework began to take on another meaning. I had found another entry now listed under "government intrusions." Homework was renamed the most covert government takeover as of yet.

With Clayton's newfound clarity, schoolbooks became innate enemies and deemed hostiles to his regime. While I was still required to maintain passing grades to ward off any attention from the nosy school officials, I would no longer be allowed reading materials and study books. All knowledge would have to be retained without the use of these wretched government-issued tools, schoolbooks. After all, education had already claimed four of Clayton's worker bees.

Struck by irony, I became a better student amid his latest idiocies.

I could either be found late night with a flashlight in hand, textbook halfway under the bed, flat on my belly, reading or sitting quietly on the floor, trying to contact the ghosts in the house, hoping that they could read chapters to me.

Time continued to march forward. Leaves changed, and snow fell.

Christmases came and went, bringing the usual fare of piled-high gifts of guilt and familiar parcels of hunting knives and bullets, all gifts for Beatrice, from a loving Clayton. Sadie visited often, though she would much rather that I meet her at the store instead. Studying the behaviors of

Clayton and Beatrice, I began to figure out the best times to sneak off to the store to be around civilization, especially on long school breaks.

Beatrice began to take me out of the house more often, her random acts of kindness. As I was older, quieter, and thought to be less of a threat, she rewarded me with short trips accompanying her on errands. Every couple of weeks, as long as my Saturday chores were done, she would offer to take me with her into town. Beatrice, always a creature of habit, would go to the same grocery store, the day-old-bread store, the feed store, and lastly to the local Woolworths for knickknacks and window-shopping.

On one particular Saturday outing, we ran into a group of card readers—charlatans, as Beatrice called them—setting up at the strip shopping center near the Grand Union where Beatrice did her grocery shopping. Somehow, I caught the eye of one particular card reader as we passed by. The woman, sensing that I wasn't allowed to speak to strangers, looked at me and then turned and smiled sweetly to Beatrice.

"Your daughter there is a healer. Do you know that? She has the gift of faith healing. Let her put her hand on whatever ails you and see if you notice the difference."

Uncomfortable at first that someone had noticed me at all, I had to admit it felt good to be seen. Being called a healer sounded like a compliment, something I could carry around for the rest of the day without having to give it back or have it taken away. Even if the devil's employees, according to Beatrice, had spoken the words, those words were still mine without any expectation of payment.

I was glad for my trip into town. This stranger, this woman, had provided an amazing gift, something I hadn't expected—hope.

Hope is like ice cream. You have to enjoy it fast; otherwise, it will melt away. Beatrice wasted no time in sharing with Clayton our little run-in with the charlatans. She scoffed at what the lady had said and hoped Clayton would find it funny as well. Looking into Clayton's eyes, I could tell that the topic struck a deep chord within him. Perhaps there was something more to Clayton besides being a very evil, awful man. Maybe he also had a connection to the other side? The thought that Clayton had intuition, the gift of foresight, made me shudder. Perhaps that was why he had never been caught. Maybe he had harnessed his gift and used it as a weapon, a powerful weapon.

Clayton's words jarred my senses, returning them back to reality, back to the dinginess and despair of my thoughts.

"Why don't you bring your little something special over here? Healing, they say? Well, I have something you can heal. We will start there and see what else arises in the process."

Both Clayton and Beatrice got a thrill out of Clayton's sense of disturbing and inappropriate humor. A powerful, ugly feeling came over me, like a dark thundercloud. If I could heal, then maybe I could hurt just as well.

Momentary feelings of raw, powerful rage stirred within me, scaring me to my senses, filling me to my very core. I would never allow those dark thoughts in. I would never be like the two of them. I wouldn't wish to hurt, and I would never be able to risk finding out either.

It was shortly after my experience with the reader that I realized that I needed a sense of direction, a more thorough game plan. The simple truth was that I had never been anywhere spatially except for the wood lots. I was unprepared to deal with the real world that I would meet someday on the other side of our property line. It was then that I began to associate traits that I wanted and respected to grocery items sold at the store. It had been the store that had connected me with the world in the first place. The store had brought in people for me to study, to watch, to observe. I would take the traits that I found likeable and apply them to the person I wanted to be someday when it was safe to become somebody.

Closing my eyes, I could walk through virtual aisles of the store, assigning traits to dry goods. Perishables were risky, as they wouldn't last forever.

Looking around my virtual store shelves, I began to associate valuable traits to products, Cans of tuna fish became a representation of faith. While they didn't cost much, tuna could fill the belly if and when meals stopped coming in. Although faith didn't seem to be paying much attention to my situation, I knew that God would be happy that I had picked tuna fish instead of candy to represent him. Using some saved-up change that I had stashed over the months, I bought a couple of cans of tuna fish to hide away under my bed.

Trying to enjoy the purer side of my father's humor, which I inherited, I decided that the cans of mixed nuts, while inviting, would represent all the good Christians at church who never wanted to get involved. Yes, mixed nuts served a higher calling, to stay on the store shelf and let someone else buy them.

Although anything canned was taboo in my house, I decided that canned vegetables needed to be in my virtual cart. I needed a healthy foundation, and looking back on the last thirteen years, I realized I had spent a lot of time working hard in dirt and soil, in the gardens. I had to be down to earth and real to myself and to others. Eventually, I was able to add a few cans of peas, corn, and beets to my character hope chest under the bed.

While stashing grocery items under one's bed might not seem like a fun thing to do for a budding teenager, I began to understand that I did have power over who I wanted to be. It didn't matter that the world around me seemed dangerous and lost, but it did matter what I added to my personality hope chest, my secret under the bed.

While the importance of a good sense of humor came disguised as fruit cocktail and canned peaches, happiness seemed best suited attached to cans of SpaghettiOs and canned ravioli. Of course, happiness had escaped me for so very long that I felt entitled and began enjoying a coveted can of this tomato bliss as often as I could afford to. Forbidden happiness came with a can opener, a spoon, and a nightlight.

Slowly, I was learning how to feel, how to test independence, how to make my own place within.

Although I had spent a lifetime around produce, there were some plants that didn't end up in our regular gardens. Clayton, always quite the entrepreneur, had begun to grow marijuana plants up on the hill. Once they were mature, he would fill the back of the pickup with them, cover them with a tarp, and bring the plants, roots and all, to hang upside down in their bedroom to dry.

On one of his many trolling and selling expeditions, Clayton had come back home with a man built like a bulldog with a menagerie of colorful tattoos up and down his arms—a rough looker who would have put up too much of a fight tumbling down the cellar stairs. Clayton decided that he would make a great party buddy instead. Rough looker not only had a taste for grain alcohol and pot but also had his own lucrative drug business on the side.

The late-night parties became louder and less predictable once pills and other drugs had been added to the mix of entertainment. For the next couple of years, the late-night world going on a wall a way became a very frightening place. Many weekends were spent curled up on the bottom of my metal closet or sitting between the wall and the bed, praying that I wouldn't get offered up as a party favor. Some of the latest and greatest best friends kept coming back again and again, in fact for several months. Other new best friends, especially those without families, were eventually put away like worn-out toys either up in the woods or some other concealed place.

One particularly boisterous lady that Clayton had picked up a year or two before from the gay bar had taken a special interest in Beatrice. Nancy was one of the favorites who probably outstayed her welcome. One day, she was gone, poof, vanished. When I asked Beatrice and Clayton where she was, they both gave me an odd look and simply said, "Nancy who?"

I was sixteen when Beatrice decided that she wanted to be girlfriends—not like the ones that shared her bed, but the kind of girlfriends who listened and had nice things to say instead of what they really felt inside. Beatrice had found a sudden need to bond, sharing her innermost secrets with me.

Quite honestly, I didn't know what was worse, being afraid of her or enduring her endless talk about how miserable her life was. Really, did she think mine was any better?

I am living proof that when your other senses become compromised and devalued, your brain finds ways to compensate for the deficiencies. I was becoming an amazing remote viewer. Simply put, I learned how to track Clayton by closing my eyes. At times, it seemed like I could feel him breathing inside of me. I felt his moods and tracked his movement. I knew when he was having a good day and when he was having a bad day. I knew where he was all the time and could actually see him walking about behind my closed eyes. Survival can be a mighty powerful motivator. Deciding on my terms, I agreed to be Beatrice's friend on one condition. I would watch her back, tell her when Clayton was on the move, and give her a full report of what his mood was at any given time. In return, she would leave me alone, period—no setting me up, no best friends, nothing. I would protect her, and she would leave me alone for the remaining two years I would be trapped there.

Well, even the best soothsayer couldn't have predicted what next came out of the mouth of a thrill-seeking Clayton. With the forecast warning of a large storm approaching our area, Clayton decided that it was the perfect time to teach me to drive. It was already spitting snow when Clayton grabbed the keys to the old station wagon and an unopened fifth of vodka, and off we went to lay the groundwork for my first time behind the wheel. A mastermind of cruelty, Clayton knew how to apply the maximum fear for minimal output.

By the time we skidded to a complete stop just feet away from where I was to turn onto the old logging road, gutted out from a too-wet summer, I was ready to snatch Clayton's already half-emptied bottle of vodka for myself. Making the left turn, I prayed that the snow, already three or four inches deep on the road, would help to pack up the holes I was preparing to take off the front end of the car.

Clayton's options were simple, as he repeated each one slowly, between swigs of vodka and Johnny Cash blaring on the radio. I could do as I was told and drive straight onto the dirt road until I reached the clearing, turn around, and then head home, or we could get stuck in some ruts, tear out the undercarriage of the car, and then freeze to death with Clayton being the last person I would ever see in this lifetime and the first in the afterlife.

I hesitated for a moment, trying to weigh the odds put in front of me. A part of me really wanted to watch Clayton freeze to death, but knowing that I would go with him to the other side scared me straight enough to make my way down the rutted obstacle course instead. Needless to say, Clayton, a completely empty fifth, and I made it home in mostly one piece, minus the wagon's front bumper.

Chapter 64

LAST TO LEAVE

As I finished out my junior year in high school, my late-night studies or lack thereof seemed to be paying off. My overly kind and slightly eccentric typing and shorthand teacher, smelling strongly of rosewater, had a very special surprise in store for her pupils. After carefully grading and reviewing our year-end skill and assessment tests, she had been granted special permission from the school district to take her business class on a weeklong, school-day-attended field trip. The next day, while traveling on the big yellow school bus to meet our temporary bosses, she began to read from the roster where we would be assigned our mock military jobs on base.

Truly God is not an angry, vindictive God. Nor is God above playing practical jokes. While my teacher held on to the back of the bus seats, steadying herself while reading out loud from her list of job assignments, it became quite clear that God had an amazing sense of humor above all else.

For my hard work and best efforts, I would be working in the legal department for one week.

Life with all its twists and turns had placed me working less than three feet away from top military attorneys. These guys had the military police on their speed dial and wielded a bigger book of rules than even Clayton. I wondered if they could pick up my scent, my years of secretiveness. What would they say if they knew they were sitting right next to the daughter of killers? A victim of sex crimes, a young girl who dried marijuana in the dryer for an impatient father who simply couldn't wait for Mother Nature to dry out his pot? Could they tell that I ate roadkill for supper and prayed every night that God wouldn't hand me a straitjacket as my eighteenth-birthday present? Fortunately for the harmony of all persons concerned, they never did. I kept busy and kept quiet.

Beatrice, increasingly curious about my school assignment, came into my bedroom as I was staring up at my ceiling in the dark. I had one more full day on base before my short military career would be over for good.

Beatrice had wanted to say no when the permission slip came home, but the fear of being questioned as to why I couldn't go seemed greater than just signing her name. Clayton would have gone crazy if he had known what his last-to-leave daughter was up to. Bad enough that I betrayed him by going to the military base in the first place but to work for someone who easily could have put him behind bars? Now that would have made him lethal.

It was disheartening that my greatest honor was also another secret, my disgrace. Beatrice could sense that it was troubling me, though it gave her a private kick that I was doing something so blatantly against Clayton.

Handing me a glass of milk, her parting words resonated out, tweaking my subconscious memory.

"Don't worry, my babe. Drink your milk, and tomorrow you won't remember anything at all. By morning, your thoughts will be forgotten. I'm counting on it."

Somewhere I had heard those same words before, yet I couldn't quite wrap my head around them. My thoughts began to grow thick, foamy, and far away. Before long, I was unable to hold my eyes open at all. Somewhere off in the distance, the pads of Beatrice's slippers could be heard lightly trailing off on the carpeted floor. Behind her steps, somewhere muffled in the distance, foil wrapping made a light tapping sound as it hit the inside of the trash can.

A. Tacked

My senior year was coming to a close, though honestly I couldn't remember much of it. Beatrice continued to quiz me each morning before school, and like that old worn-out Etch A Sketch of the past, my screen was blank, erased. Closing in on my eighteenth birthday, I began to get a little sloppy and restless with the wait for graduation day. In celebration of eighteen candles, Sadie sneaked me out for an overnight camping adventure at the local state park, five miles away.

The world is mighty big, especially when you are not sitting in a closet or under a bed to see it. Looking at the stars under a warm blanket of summer night, I knew that I was in the home stretch. Last to leave had a future and a new start on life. Settling in for a restful sleep, I prayed that morning would not find us too soon.

Coming home early Saturday morning, not yet gone twenty-four hours, I could feel the heaviness of the air in the house as soon as I opened the front door. Beatrice stared at me as if she had forgotten that she had been the one to grant me permission in the first place, lest, of course, Clayton found out.

Needless to say, that was exactly what happened. Clayton was enraged that I had been gone all night.

He would kill his slut before he would ever allow her to slink away without his permission, especially overnight.

The afternoon dragged on with an indescribable tension of silence bearing down. No one was talking. Life stood completely still. Even Ray had made himself scarce, disappearing to the safety of his shack. By the three o'clock hour, Clayton began to drink heavily, slamming the glass down hard on each new refill. I could feel a menacing threat of trouble brewing at the ready to boil over—the kind of trouble that you can't turn your back to for fear that it would overtake you, be the last thing you would ever see. It was close to six o'clock before Clayton spoke, calling me to the living room. Here I was just feet from the finish line, and I was going to get tripped up. I was going down.

Instinctively, I backed up as Clayton lunged the weight of his body toward me. Running to the kitchen, Clayton and I began an intense game of catch-me-if-you-can around and around the old metal table with the twisted legs. After nearly twenty full minutes of ducking and running in opposite directions, I gave up, stood my ground, and waited to be knocked unconscious. Clayton, a little taken aback that I was no longer running, glared at me with an intense look of disdain and hatred as we locked eyes for a moment longer before he grabbed me. It was hard to breathe with Clayton's left arm snugly around my neck. The vile smell emanating from his mouth felt heavy, making my ear damp and sticky from his lack of basic hygiene.

For the next very long several seconds, Clayton just held on tight, probably trying to administer one of those famous sleeper holds from the endless wrestling matches that he watched. For those few moments, I felt surely I was going to die. Had Clayton been planning this all along? Was this my final farewell gift that couldn't wait until graduation day? Suddenly recognizing that I wasn't asleep, Clayton began to tap my nose with his right fist, making the contact a little harder on each continuous connection.

"I'll break your fucking nose right now, you slutty tramp. Just like a fucking egg, I'll crack it just enough, slowly so you can feel the blood running down the back of your throat. Then bam, the final hit will smash your fucking nose like a busted egg yolk all over your face."

Fear and adrenaline helped to alert my basic need for survival, forcing my eyes to look around the kitchen, looking left to right for anything that would save me, anything that could help me. Catching Beatrice's shape out of my peripheral vision, I was astonished that she was actually sitting in her favorite chair, watching everything. Shifting my body weight ever so slightly, I was able to give her more of the view that she craved. I wanted her to see, to witness all the vileness she allowed because she was weak and sick, just like Clayton. I was her sacrificial lamb, as all my brothers and sisters before me had been. I wanted her to watch, to know the horror she had partnered up with.

Trying to balance out the weight of Clayton's body on my shoulder, I took a step to the side, trying to relieve some of the pressure that made the muscles in my neck feel like they were separating. Doing so, I was able to see the top of the kitchen stove, which now was just about in arm's reach. The large cast-iron frying pan used to cook up breakfast was still sitting on top of the stove, the grease now hard and smooth. I knew that I would have only one chance, one strike. Missing wouldn't be an option; it would have to be certain death.

Reaching down for the handle, I turned toward Beatrice so she could see what I had discovered. It was time to pay up; she deserved to see the frying pan moments away from her husband's skull.

"Don't do it!" Beatrice screamed loud and hard from the living room.

Clayton, jolted by the sudden outburst, loosened his grip on my neck.

Within an instant, I realized that revenge wouldn't give me peace. I had been given a moment to act, and taking it, I chose running over hitting.

Like a stray dog, I stood in the field behind our house, trying to decide which way to turn and whether to run or what to do. I had never fought back before; there were no rules for this, no set of instructions. From my vantage point, I could see that the store was still open, as customers were coming and going, completely unaware of my dire situation just yards away.

As my thoughts continued to race, I heard Beatrice's voice coming from the back porch. She sounded scared and desperate.

"Come back home now, Helen. If you don't come home right now, he will kill me. Come back! He will blame it all on me if you don't."

Somehow, that was not very reassuring to me. Still, I wasn't a monster and didn't know how to behave like one. I never wanted to come back, but no one should die on my behalf either. Honestly, that included me too.

Pacing the fields for over an hour, I tried to come to terms with what I was preparing to do. Praying that Clayton had passed out by then, I walked back to death row. I still had three weeks before high school graduation.

All the lights in the house were off when I sneaked through the back door.

Beatrice's silhouette punctuated the darkness as I watched carefully to see if she would rise from her corner, her chair. Silently she watched me too as I scanned each room, looking for Clayton. Determining that he must have passed out while I was outside, I cautiously went to my bedroom and shut the door firmly behind me.

The next morning came just as each and every morning thus far except with one obvious difference. Walking into the kitchen, afraid of a rehash of last night's performance, I soon discovered that Clayton had no interest in me at all. In fact, Clayton refused to speak to me, look at me, or recognize that he even saw me. Overnight, I had turned into a ghost as far as he was concerned. Being declared dead prematurely by Clayton was a hell of a lot better than the alternative.

Beatrice busied herself around the house, wiping up the reality of our previous night like spilled milk from the countertop. We were done, this time really done.

A couple of weeks later, Beatrice came to my graduation and watched as all of us seniors threw our funny blue graduation caps into the air together as a statement of our newly found freedoms. Little did everyone know just how much meaning actually went into that final hoorah as my cap sailed into the air, higher and farther away than all the rest.

Packing was a simple task, requiring only a cardboard box or two.

Clayton had taught me not to become attached to inanimate objects, as they could be taken away at any moment. Because of his lessons, worldly possessions meant little to me. Metaphorically speaking, if it didn't fit on the back of a dragonfly, then I didn't need it anyway. Giving the house one last glance, one last look around, I felt a sudden sense of loss, a profound sadness. The walls had held so many secrets, the others' and mine. The spirits that lived between them had not only been intruders; some had been friends. Some had sat with me when I said my prayers each night; others had stayed because they felt they had no other place to go. I would be leaving them forever, and in return, they would be leaving me as well.

There was so much pain to let go of. Could I really let it go, or would the Etch A Sketch simply store all the memories, dumping them, spilling them out when I least expected it?

All these years of praying to remain normal, to be normal—was that even possible? Could the light switch come on after all this time? Was normal different for everyone? Had the connection that I felt with the ghosts in the house been "my" normal? Would there be guidelines I could follow? Would the simple cans of food beneath my bed be enough to guide my character?

It was time to shut the door on one life, time to lock it shut while pushing the door of new beginnings wide open.

Now, opening the front door into the afternoon sunshine, I knew the next step would be into the world I would make for myself. Pausing for a moment, I shut my eyes, feeling a gentle breeze caressing the side of my cheek. Perhaps the spirits were saying good-bye to me too.

Do you see what I see? There is a rainbow shining over me. No longer in a hopeless storm, I'll be safe and warm because … *I am free*!

Many years have passed…excerpt from the next book Contemptus, the final chapters of despair in the twisted legacy of Beatrice and Clayton

Jacob was full-grown now. A bright, sensitive son, he was the apple of Sadie's eye. Her only child, her only son had turned out as good as any mother could have hoped for. She had protected him well, as best she could, from the family secrets. She would always protect him, the son who broke the cycle of despair in a life that Sadie had grown up in.

Jacob had taken the oath of honor, to serve as a public servant of the law, only wanting to do his part to keep murderers and baby rapists behind bars as long as the law would allow. He had a mission to keep innocent people safe, at least under his watch. Honor wasn't simply a code he was required to follow; it was a way of life for Jacob.

Clayton, Grandfather, or, as Jacob called him, "Pop," couldn't believe it when he heard of Jacob's plans. Rage had built up, causing the veins in his neck to practically burst inside of him. He would be done with Jacob, pure and simple. Knowing that Jacob would never carry on the legacy that he had hoped for, he kept his uncompromising promise to never speak of Jacob's name ever again.

A lot had happened, more than he had ever cared to think about. The upside-down, topsy-turvy past had revealed its ruthless self, and even now as Jacob performed CPR on his grandfather's lifeless body, he had doubts.

Life worth living came down to honor; it wasn't up to him to decide for his grandfather, nor for his grandmother, Beatrice. Jacob's job was to do what he knew was right and let the law handle the rest.

Beatrice laid the pillow back where it had originally been resting, behind Clayton's head. Her thoughts, her sanity, had scattered away to the winds months before, leaving her with only fragments and pieces of the world she once lived in with Clayton. She knew they weren't alone; in fact, the others had been the ones to remind her about the pillow. They knew that Clayton stayed drunk and abusive. It had been the others who had reminded her that drunks can't fight back, even to survive.

About the Author

A. Tacked has lived in Dallas, Texas, for thirty-five years. She has worked in the medical field for most of those years. She also teaches meditation, relaxation, and channeling and provides spiritual guidance throughout the United States.

About the Book

> Now I lay me
> down to sleep,
> I pray the Lord my soul to keep.
> If I should die
> before I wake,
> I pray the Lord
> my soul to take.
>
> But if I am to live,
> please, God, keep me
> normal.
> —Helen

Altered Grace is an autobiography written to inspire faith and hope, a testimony to the value of prayer and a tribute to the spirit that refuses to be destroyed.

Printed in the United States
By Bookmasters